E-GOVERNANCE IN INDIA

About the Author

R.P. Sinha retired from the Indian Administrative Service as Principal Adviser for Communications and Information, Planning Commission. He was Secretary to the Government of India and has held a number of important assignments in the government.

Having started his career as an academic in 1960, he has returned to this field after retirement in 2001 and is Visiting Professor in the Institute of Applied Manpower Research of the Planning Commission. The author combines academics with his vast practical experience in governance and administration. He has considerable creative contribution to the field of media arts as well besides papers and articles on a wide variety of subjects.

E-GOVERNANCE IN INDIA
Initiatives and Issues

R.P. SINHA

in collaboration with

Centre for Public Policy and Governance
INSTITUTE OF APPLIED MANPOWER RESEARCH
NEW DELHI

CONCEPT PUBLISHING COMPANY, NEW DELHI-110059

ISBN: 978-81-8069-311-3

Edition 2025

Published and Printed by

Concept Since 1974

Concept Publishing Company Pvt. Ltd.
A/15-16, Commercial Block, Mohan Garden
New Delhi-110059 (India)
T: +91-11-41101460
E: publishing@conceptpub.com, *W*: www.conceptpub.com

Cataloging in Publication--Courtesy: D.K. Agencies (P) Ltd. <docinfo@dkagencies.com>

Sinha, R. P.
E-governance in India : initiatives and issues / R.P. Sinha.
p. cm.
Includes bibliographical references (p.)
Includes index.
ISBN 8180693112

1. Internet in public administration—India.
I. Title.

DDC 352.380 285 467 8 22

Preface

E-governance is an evolving process. Conceptually, it is wider than E-government and, even though, in India, government programmes are largely for E-government the business and industry is racing to make the best use of Information and Communication Technologies (ICT) gradually ushering in the era of E-commerce. However, the scenario in India, even in the year 2K5, remains a patchwork devoid of logical progression. Technology is the enabling factor on which the new paradigm is based but the process has several non-technological dimensions as well. Government programmes have often been rolled out on the basis of technological fancies without preparing the base or conceiving the big picture.

It was around 1960 that computers came to India but it took more than three decades to harness their ever-increasing power for delivering services to the people. By their very nature, computers could not do much in serving the citizens effectively till the time when the phenomenon of networking spread wide. Networking along with computing power and large capacity for data storage led to immense possibilities that enabled governments round the globe to come to the aid of the citizens for better interaction and service deliveries. Those who reached the head of the race were not only technologically superior nations but generally had a long practice of treating the citizen service delivery as important component of government functioning. On the other hand, countries, which had authoritarian systems of governance, could not do much to make the best and effective use of the possibilities that technology placed at their doorsteps as they were hamstrung by a negative work culture.

There is a lot of scattered material available on how various governments have gone about the work of introducing E-governance. However, analysis of results and evaluation of options is not a favourite subject in academic quarters. This book seeks to put together various aspects of E-governance with special emphasis on the Indian situation. A number of fundamental issues about the feasibility of E-governance in the sense that it has appeared in advanced countries have been dealt with in a simple way. Some selected states have been taken up which may adequately represent the various stages in the process although, barring a few, most have used the centrally conceived template for E-governance.

The book is the result of the research undertaken by the author at the Institute of Applied Manpower Research. No fieldwork has been done for the collection of facts or data to test ground realities regarding the way the systems are actually working and the information available in public domain has been used. A critical evaluation of the schemes and projects initiated by various governments during the last few years involving public expenditure should be taken up by research institutions as early as possible.

I am thankful to the Centre for Public Policy and Governance for providing an opportunity for undertaking this work, which should be of use to government functionaries and planners as well as to students and IT professionals. My special thanks go to Dr. H. Ramachandran, former Director of the Institute of Applied Manpower Research for providing the motivation for such a study. The institute provided the necessary environment and facilities for collection of vast amount of material and information from diverse sources on the subject on which very little is available in printed form. I offer earnest thanks to Dr. Shailendra Sharma, present Director of the institute and my old associate for getting the work published expeditiously. I am also thankful to Shri Ashok Kumar, P. S., for helping me in the typing and production process.

New Delhi
15 September, 2005

R.P. Sinha

Contents

One

Good Governance and E-Governance

The last decade of the twentieth century saw a very rapid development and spread of Information and Communication Technologies (ICT) along with the advent of user-friendly computing systems and networking. These new technologies have placed a powerful tool in the hands of the society that could be used to make life easier and better for all in several dimensions of human activities. Almost all areas of social and commercial activity have been touched by the electronic revolution. Governments have been quick to pick up its applications for providing better information and services to the people. Business and Industry have come to depend on the new applications in a big way. In spite of the vast differences in the levels and degree of use of electronics in government in the global and regional context the feeling that the world is marching towards 'E-governance age' is unmistakable.

Use of electronics in government and business started more than forty years ago. Automation in production processes, computerised record keeping and data management grew vastly over the years. The advent of the Personal Computer (PC) has, in fact, brought about a revolution in the way work is transacted at public and private offices. Governments have improved their systems of delivery of information and services through Information Technology (IT) applications and networking. In the global scenario the extent of use of IT in government and governance varies considerably from country to country and even in different parts of countries but there is a continuing process of innovations and trials. No country has brought in E-governance fully and completely yet although E-government situations are fairly advanced in many countries.

Governance and Good Governance

The institution of government, in some form or the other, has existed since the dawn of history and has acted as an important tool of civilisation of mankind and governance has been practised since times immemorial. However, 'good governance' is an evolving concept that has become increasingly relevant in the present societies all over the world.

There is no agreed or settled definition of 'governance' but it is understood as a process. Webster's Third International Dictionary (1986) makes governance synonymous with government as also 'the act or process of governing, specifically authoritative direction and control'. The concept of 'governance' goes beyond that of 'government' which may not involve the citizens at all and yet do all that is necessary for the orderly existence of a society.

In recent years the concern for 'good governance' arising out of studies undertaken by the World Bank and other international donor agencies have prompted scholars to conceptualise governance in a wider context. In that approach, political legitimacy issues have led to the concept of governance as 'the conscious management of regime structures, with a view to enhancing the public realm'.

According to Goram Hyden governance is a rational concept, emphasising the nature of interactions between state and social actors, and among social actors themselves.

The concept of 'government', in a broad sense, is that of a mechanism or institution to enforce order and control through the core functions of *legislation, execution* and *adjudication*. As against this, the evolving concept of 'governance' encompasses *markets, hierarchies* and *networks*. The wider connotation and use of the term 'governance' reflects a blurring of the distinction between the state and the 'civil society' leading to the view that civil society determines the principles for interaction in the populace, not just the government, including the empowerment process and linkages. In the advanced concept governance is defined as the ability of people to take greater control over their own development.

Many functions of the government involve delivery of information and services to its citizens. In some countries governments have progressively taken upon themselves larger and larger responsibilities in the name of welfare and common good. In such situations occasions of interaction with bureaucracy in the life of a citizen multiply. This invariably leads to corruption and entrenchment of bureaucracy. In these societies government and governance have overlapping association. Any improvement in government-citizen interaction or creation of improved facilities for such interaction, even in matters like payment of revenues or dues of government owned utilities, is seen as improvement in governance whereas this is only the beginning of good governance.

The World Bank has laid great stress on the state of governance since there is a link between growth and good governance. In many developing countries, including India, resources pumped in for development and growth have failed to produce the extent of results envisaged because of bad governance.

According to Kofi A. Annan, Secretary General of the United Nations, "Good governance is perhaps the single most important factor in eradicating poverty and promoting development."

The traditional concept of good governance is taken to mean the rule of law, fight against poverty, better management of the state's resources, control of corruption and respect for human rights. But with globalisation, reforms, changing concepts and increasing role of market the concept of good governance transcends the state by taking on board the private sector and civil society in addition to the government. The state creates a conducive political and legal environment and the private sector generates economic activity and growth for creating incomes and employment. The civil society facilitates political and social interaction by mobilising groups to participate in economic, social and political activities.

The UNDP has defined governance as the exercise of economic, political and administrative authority to manage a country's affairs at all levels, comprising the mechanisms, processes and institutions through which that authority is directed. Good governance is, among other things, participatory, transparent, accountable and efficient. It recognises that governance is exercised by the private sector and civil society as well as the state, all of which have important roles to play in promoting sustainable human development. It is also effective and equitable. And it promotes the rule of law. Good governance ensures that political, social and economic priorities are based on broad consensus in society and that the voices of the poorest and the most vulnerable are heard in decision-making over the allocation of development resources. It has recently (1998) revamped its policy document reflecting the fact that more than a third of its programming budget is now earmarked for activities in governance.

In the process of rendering financial assistance, technical support and policy advice the International Monetary Fund (IMF) also lays great emphasis on good governance by helping countries ensure the rule of law, improve the efficiency and accountability of their public sectors and tackle corruption.

Indicators of Governance

The World Bank has developed six indicators of governance and about 175 countries have been studied and comparisons made to reach some conclusions about the factors of governance that affect growth and development. These indicators are:

- Voice and Accountability
- Political Stability/No Violence
- Government Effectiveness
- Regulatory Quality
- Rule of Law
- Control of Corruption

The first two factors involve political and ideological dimensions and are not being reckoned here. Rule of Law is well structured in many countries including India. The three remaining factors are of interest in our understanding of good governance and the impact on development. Table 1 gives a comparison of the 'Government Effectiveness' across selected countries in terms of their percentile ranking that may have some relevance to India. Table 2 gives similar comparisons for 'Regulatory Quality' and Table 3 gives the figures for 'Control of Corruption'.

Table 1: Government Effectiveness, Comparison Across Selected Countries

Country	*Dataset*	*Percentile Rank (0-100)*	*Standard Deviation*	*Number of surveys/polls*
Brazil	2000-01	44.3	0.18	9
Canada	2000-01	95.6	0.19	9
China	2000-01	57.6	0.18	9
France	2000-01	86.7	0.19	8
India	2000-01	48.1	0.18	9
Japan	2000-01	84.2	0.19	9
Malaysia	2000-01	69.0	0.19	9
United Kingdom	2000-01	96.2	0.18	10
United States	2000-01	93.0	0.19	9

Source: D. Kaufmann and A. Kraay, 2002: Growth without Governance.

Table 2: Regulatory Quality, Comparison Across Selected Countries

Country	*Dataset*	*Percentile Rank (0-100)*	*Standard Deviation*	*Number of surveys/polls*
Brazil	2000-01	50.3	0.27	7
Canada	2000-01	88.6	0.29	6
China	2000-01	40.1	0.27	7
France	2000-01	74.9	0.29	6
India	2000-01	37.7	0.27	7
Japan	2000-01	76.6	0.27	6
Malaysia	2000-01	55.7	0.29	6
United Kingdom	2000-01	96.4	0.27	7
United States	2000-01	95.2	0.27	7

Source: D. Kaufmann and A. Kraay, 2002: Growth without Governance.

Table 3: Control of Corruption, Comparison Across Selected Countries

Country	Dataset	Percentile Rank (0-100)	Standard Deviation	Number of surveys/ polls
Brazil	2000-01	56.6	0.17	10
Canada	2000-01	95.6	0.19	9
China	2000-01	48.4	0.16	10
France	2000-01	84.3	0.19	8
India	2000-01	44.0	0.16	10
Japan	2000-01	86.8	0.17	10
Malaysia	2000-01	61.6	0.18	9
United Kingdom	2000-01	94.3	0.18	10
United States	2000-01	91.2	0.19	9

Source: D. Kaufmann and A. Kraay, 2002: Growth without Governance.

Legacy Structures of Governance

It is worth noting that those countries which have remained under colonial rule and have gained independence in the middle of the twentieth century have the legacy structure of public administration which, in the first place, was never designed to act as machinery for growth and development. It had no primary concern for the convenience or the involvement of the citizens. The situation, in many cases, only deteriorated and governance suffered in the years following independence. India is a typical example where, in spite of all capabilities, government-citizen interaction became increasingly painful and unfriendly over the years. Development efforts suffered due to corruption and inefficiency in the system. The hallmark of government bureaucracy at all levels has been a tendency to hide information from the citizen and convert this into a tool of harassment and extraction of illegal gratification. In India, although there have been some feeble attempts at bringing about administrative reforms, the ground realities have hardly changed. It has, in fact, become worse with the rules and procedures continuing to be loaded in favour of those who administer the affairs rather than the citizen.

Most of the problems that the citizen faces in interacting with the government and its numerous agencies relate to:

- Complexity of procedure
- Getting access to a functionary who can really decide the issue
- Tendency of the functionaries to ask for information piece-meal
- Lack of transparency in the method of decision-making
- Uncertainty about the time frame of processing the case
- Slow and inefficient working
- Holding back communication even after decision

Most of these issues of attitude and work-methods can be handled with improvement in procedures and tackling improper attitudes. The two, namely, procedures and attitudes, are, however, not inseparable and could converge to cause comfort or annoyance to the citizen. Good and helpful behaviour, transparent method of decision-making and a concern for the citizen can appreciably take out the frustrating consequences and pain of cumbersome procedures.

In many situations the equipment, tools and internal procedures can make a big difference. Office equipments like photocopying machines, Fax, filing systems, yellow slips, organiser, diaries, etc. could make a lot of difference in the productivity of functionaries which, in turn, have effect on the delivery speed of the service. The advent of business machines began transforming management both in the business and the government and the use of computers and ICT is a culmination of that process with unprecedented outcomes that have opened up new dimensions of interactivity between government and the citizen that was seen never before.

Good Governance and E-Governance

Improving governance should be a natural objective of governments. Modern governments all over the world have tried to provide what may be called good government through introduction of management techniques into public administration. In many developed countries tools and aids available at various times were put to best use to improve delivery systems. Developing countries have also made efforts, due to necessity often arising out of public pressures, to improve or for sheer imitation of something in vogue, a tendency that is seen even in the matter of introducing E-government and E-governance. The power of ICT tools have opened up possibilities much beyond the 'improvement' syndrome by permitting radical possibilities in decision-making, quick processing of data and information transfer by automated electronic methods instantly. Internet, which was born out of public funding and through government institutions, was universalised by its immense commercial possibilities and total freedom to grow and expand.

The power of ICT has permitted governments to adopt a 'linked-up' or 'holistic' approach by connecting various departments and organs of government as never before. It has also provided external linkages facilitating exchange of information with other organs of the civil society and in turn disseminating information and data universally.

In the earlier stages of E-government the internal functioning of the government was assisted by electronic methods. These have gradually taken over the external functioning also and the efficiencies generated through computerisation and limited networking in the earlier stages have been extended to the government's delivery systems.

The transformation usually takes place in the following stages:

- Improvement in referencing and filing systems in paper laden offices
- Use of computers for storage and processing of data
- Linking of computers in Local Area Networks and Wide Area Networks
- Geographical penetration of connectivity in rural and remote areas
- Connectivity through Internet and Intranet
- Opening of public service outlets for information and simple services
- Using ICT for decision-making in the government

Non-governmental agencies including business, industry, educational and research institutions have taken to ICT in a much more pervasive fashion and there the proliferation has been much faster than in governments.

E-government does not necessarily require public involvement in determining or shaping the manner of service deliveries although they are created for the benefit of the citizens who are treated like customers. In the E-government models generally followed there is considerable reduction of 'internal organisational friction'. Networks are an important organ of the systems, but it is the ability of the internet and intranets to 'join up' and coordinate the activities of previously disparate government departments and services that is seen as the most important feature of E-government.

The further use of ICT has led to what is described as E-governance the intimate dimensions of which include E-commerce, E-democracy and E-citizen. Democracies have different models but ideological aspirations could not be put into practice even if there was political will and legitimacy since interaction with citizens was only a legal fiction that was attained through the institution of 'people's representatives'. Even the best functioning democracies manifest only through the process of elections or the rare phenomenon of referendum. The electronic tools and networking have made it possible to involve the 'citizen' in decision-making. E-democracies can carve a much larger role for the citizen. This can only be an ultimate objective towards which some governments may progress whiles others may not. From the technological and administrative angle, such stage would require the presence of the 'capability of consultation' through a two-way communication channel between the government and the citizen. Such a paradigm has been made possible through ICT and there is no technological barrier of a kind that may deny the citizen easy access to the governmental processes. Consultative interaction has been made possible for all levels of activities beginning from the details of the service outputs to serious policy issues or even emergency issues like natural catastrophe or war. Whether this will actually happen is dependent not on limitations of technology but on the will of the people and those who represent the will in the present paradigm of governance.

Two

E-Governance Status in the World

The notion of E-governance has its roots in attempts in many countries to 'modernise' government in response to perceived citizen dissatisfaction or disengagement. Internationally, application of Information and Communication Technologies (ICT) to the internal functioning of the governments and for service delivery to citizens is at different stages. Although there is a growing feeling that ICT in government and governance offers almost limitless possibilities like evolving new forms of citizenship, the technologies have not been fully harnessed even in the countries leading the global E-governance scenario. The notable fact is that the literature on E-governance is always much ahead of the actual achievements.

Acceding to Kate Oakley, there are at least three different models of E-government:

- ***The 'New Economy' model*** that stresses the similarities between E-government and E-business focusing on delivering high quality public services and on moving to a more 'self-service' citizenship, which over time will shrink the size of the state. It is also seen as a regional and local tool for economic development where the development of infrastructure tends to follow the market. This invariably leads to 'digital divide.' The US, New Zealand and the UK are the examples of this model.

- ***The 'E-community' model*** that is more favoured in continental European societies, particularly those such as the Netherlands or Scandinavian countries which have a strong tradition of civil society and freedom of information, high levels of education and technology penetration and a relatively even distribution of wealth. This model stresses potential social innovations resulting from widespread access and the role of citizens as co-producers of services.
- ***The 'planned economy' model*** that is used in countries such as Singapore or Malaysia, which traditionally use interventionist public sector tools to drive and shape private sector activity and investment. As in the 'new economy' model, economic development is very much a driver, but the development of IT and communication infrastructure and the skills to use it is seen as a government responsibility.

According to Hunter, "citizens expectations of government have been permanently altered in recent years by forces such as: aging populations, increased service expectations, security concerns, a talent crunch, competition by the private sector and fiscal pressure that forces governments to find ways to do more with less. End-to-end E-government transactions are emerging as one of the most promising tools for governments to use in achieving real transformation as they deliver public services in the 21st century."

The pace at which governments are taking to ICT varies greatly due to factors like lack of financial and human resources, conservatism, no genuine desire to make the government transparent and often public criticism that the benefits of E-governance flow only to the elitist segments of the society. Even amongst the achievers, the picture is often exaggerated.

In a study conducted jointly by the United Nations Division for Public Economics and Public Administration (UNDPEPA) and American Society for Public Administration (ASPA) to present E-governance environment and landscape of its member countries and benchmark core areas endemic to national E-governance programmes, it was found that out of 190 nations surveyed, only 17 had on-line transaction capacity. Government websites, not necessarily national governmental websites, were found only in the case of 169 countries indicating that about 21 countries do not have even a static information dissemination system through Internet.

The Commonwealth Network of Information Technology for Development (COMNET-IT) and UNESCO have conducted global survey, published in the year 2000, which was further followed up with detailed profiles of 15 countries, including India. Impact of E-governance in the commercial, NGO and professional areas was covered in these studies, with special focus on specific government initiatives, such as:

- Liberalization of telecommunications
- Development of cyber laws
- Plans for E-government
- Plans for the development of an info-society
- Deployment of community E-centres
- Instances of public feedback to statements of direction, draft legislation, etc.
- Web-sites of government agencies, particularly if these offer value beyond a public relations image.

In another comprehensive study undertaken by The Economic Intelligence Unit, Pyramid Research, rankings for 'E-readiness' have been developed. The US, predictably, comes out at the first place. Australia takes second place, putting English-speaking countries in the top four slots, with the UK placed third and Canada, fourth. Surprisingly, India, with all its aggressive global presence of IT professionals, ranks 45th. The list below gives the complete Pyramid rankings with the scores shown after the hyphen:

E-business Leaders

1. US-8.73
2. Australia-8.29
3. UK-8.10

4. Canada-8.09
5. Norway-8.07
6. Sweden-7.98
7. Singapore-7.87
8. Finland-7.83
9. Denmark-7.70
10. Netherlands-7.69
11. Switzerland-7.67
12. Germany-7.51
13. Hong Kong-7.45

E-business Contenders

14. Ireland-7.28
15. France-7.26
16. (tie)-Austria-7.22
17. (tie)-Taiwan-7.22
18. Japan-7.18
19. Belgium-7.10
20. New Zealand-7.00
21. South Korea-6.97
22. Italy-6.74
23. Israel-6.71
24. Spain-6.43
25. Portugal-6.21

E-business Followers

26. Greece-5.85
27. Czech Republic-5.71
28. Hungary-5.49
29. Chile-5.28
30. Poland-5.05
31. Argentina-5.01
32. Slovakia-4.88
33. Malaysia-4.83

34. Mexico-4.78
35. South Africa-4.74
36. Brazil-4.64
37. Turkey-4.51
38. Colombia-4.24
39. Philippines-3.98
40. (tie)-Egypt-3.88
41. (tie)-Peru-3.88
42. Russia-3.84
43. Sri Lanka-3.82
44. Saudi Arabia-3.80
45. India-3.79
46. Thailand-3.75
47. Venezuela-3.62

Lagging Behind

48. Bulgaria-3.38
49. China-3.36
50. (tie)-Ecuador-3.30
51. (tie)-Iran-3.30
52. (tie)-Romania-3.20
53. (tie)-Ukraine-3.20
54. (tie)-Algeria-3.16
55. (tie)-Indonesia-3.16
56. Nigeria-2.91
57. Kazakhstan-2.76
58. Vietnam-2.76
59. Azerbaijan-2.72
60. Pakistan-2.66

Source: The EIU E-business forum

The position of China at 49, in the near company of Iran, is another surprising fact, which indicates that China, in spite of growth and progress in several areas, is yet to create conditions conducive to E-business.

Another survey conducted by The World Markets Research Center indicates that full technological potential of the internet is not being used by governments even in the leading countries. The survey studied 2,288 national government websites in 196 nations. Among the sites analyzed were executive offices, legislative offices, judicial offices, Cabinet offices, and government agencies involved in health, taxation, education, economic development, foreign affairs, foreign investment, tourism and business regulation. It was found that USA scored only 57.2 per cent as the highest-ranking nation. Taiwan and Australia ranked second and third with 52.5 and 50.7 per cent, with Canada and the UK in fourth and fifth positions.

The survey indicated that, worldwide, the level of E-government and E-governance is falling short of the true potential. The summary of the findings regarding the websites were:

- Privacy policies were made known only in the case of 6 per cent websites
- Only 3 per cent have a public security policy
- Only 8 per cent offered services that were fully executable on-line
- Only 6 per cent of websites have links to a government portal
- Only 33 per cent of websites provide facility for searching, which limits the ability of ordinary citizens to find relevant information quickly

Let us take a look at some selected countries to have a picture of the initiatives and methods used in those countries and also the services available. Since the E-based services are expanding at a fast rate, the information may not be the latest. However, it indicates, broadly, the range of the levels of electronic governance in the world.

Australia

First Phase: Online Services

In 1997, the Australian Government decided that all appropriate Federal Government services would be provided online by 2001. The

Government Online Strategy, released in April 2000, which mainly involved the migration of existing information services to the online environment, helped guide and assist federal agencies working towards meeting this target. The strategy involved complementing-not replacing-existing written, telephone, fax and counter services. Federal agencies responded to the challenge of placing all appropriate services online.

In February 2002, the Australian Prime Minister announced at the World Congress on Information Technology in Adelaide that this target had been met. There were in excess of 1600 government services and information sources available online and all agencies had met the important target of having all appropriate services online by December 2001. Departments and agencies also progressed well in meeting minimum standards and guidelines. Government E-procurement operations were also well advanced. According to a number of independent reports, the Australian Government's use of the Internet to provide services and programmes online is amongst the world's best.

According to Australia's National Office for the Information Economy, the efficiency gains of 'real time' interaction with government are far reaching. For example, a growing number of forms are being filled in online, saving business (in particular, small business) time and money. The extensive use of the Business Entry Point website also demonstrates that the business community recognises the benefits of government services delivered through the Internet. Over 40 per cent of the traffic to the Business Entry Point occurs outside normal working hours and at weekends.

Innovative government services, such as the Australian Taxation Office's electronic Income Tax return lodgement facility (E-tax), are becoming popular as more and more people are adopting it for their tax assessment and payments. By early November, 2002 more than 5,40,000 people had lodged their return for the year using E-tax. showing a 52 per cent increase on last year's numbers. The tax office is processing almost 100 per cent of E-tax returns within 14 days with nearly 90 per cent processed within 10 days. An online survey of E-tax users showed that 94 per cent said they would use it again in 2003.

Second Phase: Better Services Better Government

The second phase strategy, *Better Services, Better Government,* adopted in November 2002, maps out the next phase of the Federal Government's drive to move from placing government information and services online to more comprehensive and integrated application of new technologies to government information, service delivery and administration. Federal departments and agencies must move beyond the first stage of Internet applications to an even more advanced stage—the era of full-fledged E-government—in which the application of new technologies to government services, information and administration demonstrates sustained benefits to citizens, business and government itself.

This strategy maps out the policy framework within which federal departments and agencies will go about achieving that objective. The responsibility for overseeing future developments, particularly involving those where collaboration between agencies is required, will rest with the newly established Information Management Strategy Committee (IMSC) of Secretaries and CEOs from key departments and agencies.

The following six key objectives have been stated:

(i) Achieve greater efficiency and a return on investment;
(ii) Ensure convenient access to government services and information;
(iii) Deliver services that are responsive to client needs;
(iv) Integrate related services;
(v) Build user trust and confidence;
(vi) Enhance closer citizen engagement.

Federal departments and agencies will continue to identify and implement online services which demonstrate real benefits. Increasingly, business will also be able both to get government business opportunities and to receive payments online. In these ways, many of the efficiency gains from E-government will flow directly to the business bottom line.

In this new era of E-government, citizens are at the core of the process. Online services are a part of a comprehensive redesign of government service delivery. For government agencies, service delivery now entails managing multiple delivery channels. Services will still be delivered through traditional means such as by telephone, fax or counter services. The overall goal though is to improve the quality of services across the board, and reduce the costs of both using and providing services. The community will also benefit from improved convenience. as many federal agencies will in effect be available to the public 24-hours-a-day, seven-days-a-week. Australians well not need to know about the structure of government in order to be able to deal effectively with it.

Government Portal

The richness, and user friendliness of the government portal (*http://www.fed.gov.au/KSP*) can only be assessed by actually visiting it. It has separate gateways for individuals, students, business and non-residents. The portal helps with information at every stage and guides the procedures with the users perspective in front. Some of the information posted is truly amazing if we compare it with the approach and the situation prevailing in countries like India. For example, the page on job search (*http://www.jobsearch.gov.au/*) gives up-to-date details of the number of jobs available region-wise, with a link to 'today's new jobs', as shown below (22 Jan. 2003):

State/Territory	*Jobs*
New South Wales	10821
Queensland	7795
Victoria	8171
Tasmania	458
Western Australia	2516
South Australia	2771
Northern Territory	457
A.C.T.	615
National Defence Jobs	413
Today's New Jobs	

From the Australian Portal *(http://www. jobsearch.gov.au/)*

E-democracy

Being one of the leading countries in E-governance, Australia is now embarking on the 'E-democracy' field. It is the responsibility of government to expand the channels of communication to reach as many citizens as possible. The Internet, though not inherently democratic, can be of great utility for aiding democratic processes. The National Office of the Information Economy of Australia, which coordinates E-government, is taking up the issue of online citizen interaction through online consultation, and in the development of policies and strategies to allow people to 'better engage with government'. At the regional level, for Queensland, which has a small population of around 3 million people, 'E-Democracy Three Year Trial' was approved by Cabinet and assigned to the Community Engagement Division, to follow the measurable and identifiable outcomes.

The Queensland Government's commitment for the next three years is to:

- post a number of issues on the website on which the government desires wide consultation and feedback;
- provide online access to government consultation documents relevant to those issues, such as discussion and policy papers and draft bills;
- broadcast Parliamentary debates over the Internet; and
- develop a system to accept petitions to the Queensland Parliament online.

In Australia, experimentation with government-led online consultation and hosting of citizen discussions has been put in practice, mostly at the state levels, web forums create talking points like *<http://www.talkingpoint.sa.gov.au>* hosted by the State of South Australia. In Victoria, an experiment called 'Have Your Say' *<http://www.haveyoursay.vic.gov. au/discussion/>* is to be incorporated as a feature of the main E-government portal.

United States of America

The Government of US is transforming its functions to focus on the needs of citizens and business alliances. As electronic commerce and "e-business" transactions became commonplace providing for end-to-end transactions, the demands for 'electronic government' increased.

E-Government approach in America is based on seven principles comprising the following:

- Easy access
- Re-engineered Systems
- Automated Systems
- One-Stop Service
- Service by Customer, not Provider
- Privacy protected and embraced
- Access to the physically challenged

A Task Force was set-up in July 2001 which considered over 160 E-government proposals and narrowed them down to 30. The President's Management Council selected 23 of the 30 cross-agency E-government initiatives for funding, and added *a payroll processing initiative* making it '24 initiatives' for E-government. Implementation road map was prepared by multi-agency project teams.

The 24 initiatives spelt out by the government in October 2002 were:

1. Recreation One Stop
2. Eligibility Assistance Online
3. Online Access for Loans
4. USA Services (Enable citizens to personalize the combination of services)
5. EZ Tax Filing (Internet fact of filing and refund)
6. Online Rule-making Management
7. Expanding Electronic Tax Products for Businesses
8. Federal Asset Sales
9. International Trade Process Streamlining

10. One-Stop Business Compliance Information
11. Geospatial Information One-Stop (resources shared)
12. e-Grants
13. Disaster Assistance and Crisis Response
14. Wireless Public Safety Interoperable Communications—Project SAFECOM
15. e-Vital
16. e-Training
17. Recruitment One-Stop
18. Integrated Human Resources
19. e-Clearance
20. e-Payroll/HR (Payroll Processing Consolidation)
21. e-Travel
22. Integrated Acquisition Environment
23. Electronic Records Management
24. e-Authentication

Use of computers and networking had been initiated much earlier in government and business but this set of initiatives has put all the efforts in a perspective and an open roadmap is available.

Some new Legislative measures and time bound action mandates have been introduced in the recent years to provide the necessary environment and push. Government-wide Mandates include:

(a) *Government's Paperwork Elimination Act of 1998* (GPEA): Agencies must offer electronic services/transactions as alternative to paper by October 2003;
(b) *Electronic Signatures in Global and National Commerce Act of 1999 (E-SIGN):* Electronic signature may not be denied legal effect; all commercial, interstate contracts, transactions, and writings may be executed electronically;
(c) Health Information Protection and Accountability Act (HIPAA);
(d) E-Grants; and
(e) EBT Interoperability Act.

The Office of Electronic Government and Technology within the Office of Government-wide Policy in the General Services Administration was formerly named the Office of Electronic Commerce and Office of Electronic Government. Adoption of E-Commerce is well-underway in Federal agencies. Government use of Internet-based services, for electronic purchasing and information sharing is becoming more sophisticated. However, a recent report published by GSA's Office of Intergovernmental Solutions noted that on-line citizen transactions are still in the early stages.

Government Portal

The official portal of the US government (*http://www.firstgov.gov/*) offers a large number of services to citizens, business and government employees. The coverage is extensive and exhaustive and the user is able to get all relevant information at one point. There are three on-line services as below:

Gateway for Citizens

On-line services for citizens consist of Free On-line Tax filing. Sale of government owned (including seized) vehicles, boats etc. Disaster help, Finding government benefits, Finding a government job, Social Security on-line, Student's loans, Passport applications, Driver's Licence, Birth and Death certificates, Recreation, Lottery results, Nursing Home comparisons, etc.

Gateway for Business

On-line services for Business include: Business opportunities, Business Laws and regulations, Central contractor registration, Government auctions and sales, E-filing of tax returns, Wage reporting, Small business procurement registration, subcontracting opportunities, filing patents and trade marks, and an Export portal.

Gateway for Government Employees

Federal and Regional Pay Tables, Per Diem rates, E-training initiatives for Federal government employees, Grants, For sale to Government buyers, Employee directory, pay-roll changes and background investigation application, etc.

This government portal also provides information and assistance in respect of loan and investments in savings bonds, treasury bills, coins, mortgage from home buyers and home owners, real estate sale offering by State and Federal agencies, gift and memorabilia mementos from museums, Presidential libraries, reservation of parks and other historical sites, Digital maps in data from US geological survey, aeronautical charts, helicopter root charts, terminal air charts, flood maps, forest services maps, national parks, train tickets, special sales for government and non-profit organizations, supply of office furniture, computers and other items for non-profit buyers, business and trading counselling, business expansion, overseas private investment, daily weather etc.

Although there is a rush to apply technology in government, significant confusion exists over a precise definition of E-government. There are no proven methods or tools yet to measure its impact on improving the quality of services to the taxpayer.

Japan

Computerisation in government in Japan started many years ago and using of computers had become quite pervasive by the mid-nineteen nineties. In December 1997, the Cabinet decided on a Revised Basic Plan for the Computerisation of Government Administration to initiate 'E-government'. In November 2000, the Basic Law for Formation of an Advanced Information-Communication Network Society was enacted. Several steps were taken thereafter for mapping out

- e-Japan Strategy
- e-Japan Priority Plan
- e-Japan 2002

The 'IT Headquarters' was installed within the Cabinet in January 2001 in accordance with the Basic IT Law and was headed by the Prime Minister himself. The IT Headquarters consisted of all Cabinet Ministers and several well-informed independent persons. The objectives before this top level body was to:

- Create Basic Policies for Measures to Accomplish Objectives
- Enhanced contents
- Form advanced information-communication networks of the highest level in the world
- Enhance ability of the people for utilization of information and fostering of experts
- Regulatory reform and promotion of e-commerce through rational protection and utilization of intellectual property
- Promotion of E-government (Enhanced simplification, efficiency and transparency of administration)
- Assured safety and reliability of networks and protection of private information
- Promotion of creative research and development
- International cooperation and contribution

A comprehensive review of procedures, speeding up of the implementation of plans and projects than what was originally planned, and widespread use of electronic systems for quicker completion of administrative processing were the important actions that were taken to give full meaning to the use of ICT in the government systems and for facilitating the interaction between the citizen and the government.

Linking the networks of the local governments with those of the central government and the other agencies of the government including public corporations ensured systemic synergies.

Japan aimed at creating an Advanced Information-Communication Network Society, with the ability of the people to effectively utilize information. The aim was to have advanced information-communication networks of the highest level in the world with proper safety and reliability of networks and systems to protect private information. It was envisaged that by March 2004, information in the computers and networks and the processing processes would equal that on the paper.

The services already available to the citizens are in the field of electronic payment of taxes and fees, matters related to motor vehicles and driving licences, Electronic Processing of Applications, Reports and Other Procedures, availability of administrative information easily accessed, 24 hours a day through homepages on the Internet, submission and opening of bids through the Internet, One-Stop Service in several areas.

It remains to be seen whether Japan is able to create administration that will equalize electronic information with paper information as planned. Steps are yet to be taken towards effective E-democracy.

Mentioned below are a few other cases, narrating very briefly regarding their approach to E-governance from the world scenario.

What Initiatives are Promoting Change in Canada?

Work done across government on the following medium-term initiatives is promoting change in response to public demand for better and move accessible government:

- *Citizen-centred Service Delivery*—improving access to services and improving client satisfaction.
- *Government of Canada On-Line*—giving Canadians secure, reliable on-line access to federal services.
- *Modern Comptrollership*—integrating financial and non-financial performance information, implementing soul rid risk management, ensuring appropriate control systems, and updating related management policies.
- *Improved Reporting to Parliament*—improving the quality of information provided to Parliamentarians on programs and results.
- *Programme Integrity*—ensuring existing programs are adequately structured and resourced.
- *Developing an Exemplary Workplace*—creating a workplace

that fosters the leadership and participation necessary to deliver on this agenda for management change.

It would be interesting to sample the strategic thrusts in the matter of bringing E-government and E-governance in some other countries, just to have a glimpse of the global thought and methods that are being practiced and which have brought changes in governance in many countries in the world.

Denmark

Denmark falls at the ninth position in the E-business listing. The approach to E-government in Denmark is based on the following principles:

- Information Society for All
- Realisation of the Global Research Village
- Realisation of Broadband internet for Research Institutions
- Use of On-line Publications
- IT Usage in Municipalities
- IT Usage in Danish Companies
- Electronic Filing
- The Portable Revolution
- IT Usage in Education
- Electronic Supported Administration and Legal Roles
- IT and the Disabled-Plan of Action

Source: *http://www.cdcinocracy.gov.uk/*

Finland

E-government in Finland is based on the following main approach and deployments:

- Sharing of Data between National Base Registers
- Messaging e-mail
- EDI for some applications

- E-commerce
- Telework
- Smart Card Use, Kiosks and Internet Use
- One-Stop Service
- Communication and Documentation become increasingly electronic

Source: *http://www.edeiTiocracy.gov.uk/*

Cyprus

Government Strategic Direction has been defined to realize the following:

- Establish Cyprus as business center for the Eastern Mediterranean
- Access to the EU
- Public Service Reform Plan
- Computerisation Plan: One Computer Terminal Per Desk; Paperless Office
- Distributed Services to the Public and Commerce; Communication Data maintained in one place
- Global Communication

Source: *http://www.edemocracv.gov.uk/*

Three

Government and IT – Indian Approach

Advent of Computers

Computers came to India in 1959 but were slow to catch on. There was a feeling amongst employees of the establishments introducing computers in the initial stages that it would replace workers and result in loss of jobs. In the course of time, the advantages became apparent and the computer started getting used in government and private sector, sporadically. In 1975, the Government of India took a conscious decision about introducing use of computers in the government and computer-based decision support system in the ministries and departments to facilitate planning and programme implementation.

Within a short time, a high priority Plan scheme was taken up and with UNDP assistance, National Informatics Centre (NIC) was set up under the Electronics Commission. The NIC contributed immensely to the growth of the computer culture in the government and it has become synonymous with computerisation in the government. It has brought 'E-government' to India through networking and computer proliferation in the various organs of the government and has been instrumental in steering Information and Communication Technology (ICT) applications in the government departments at Central, State and District levels.

NICNET

During 1985-90, a period before the spread of the Internet, NIC reached out to 550 district headquarters in the country covering different terrains and varied levels of regional development. In order to provide to specific needs for improving government services, NIC established a nationwide ICT Network called NICNET with gateway nodes at about 55 points in government departments, 35 in States/ Union Territory headquarters and 550 in district headquarters. The NICNET is first of its kind among the developing countries using the Ku-band VSAT technology.

In 1989, the committee on Study Group on Information Gap, constituted by the Planning Commission recommended creation of databases on Plan Information, Monitoring and Evaluation in districts. This committee also recommended creating databases on natural resources, infrastructure, agro-economic and demographic aspects at the district level. Based on the NICNET, the District Government Informatics Programme (DISNIC) was taken up in 540 districts. Through this programme, a distributed database on village level information has been created for about 6 lakh villages of the country.

National Task Force on IT

When the use of ICT in the governments all over the world started growing at an explosive pace and internet spread like a wild fire, keeping in mind the capabilities that India possessed in terms of human resource and market potential, the Government of India saw the possibilities and need of giving a push to the IT industry and the applications in a big way. In May 1998, the Prime Minister's Office set up a National Task Force on IT and Software Development under the Chairmanship of the Deputy Chairman of Planning Commission. This task force had a mandate to formulate the draft of a National Informatics Policy.

In its Basic Background Report, made in June 1998, the Task Force suggested as follows:

- Each department/agency in government should be required to prepare an Information Technology Plan with a time perspective of three to five years. This is necessary for planning out applications systematically.
- At least 2 per cent of the budget of every ministry or department be earmarked to apply IT in that department. This will include not only investment in the machines but also training.
- The National Informatics Centre at the national level and the Technology Service Organisations at the state level should, on the lines of the CCTA in the UK, immediately establish 'Framework Contracts' with reputed suppliers to provide a wide range of IT consultancy, specialist services and IT products to government agencies.
- As it will be difficult to train a whole lot of government servants in IT quickly, the private sector computer companies must be called upon to provide equipment as well as services. It would be useful for India to participate in international projects so as to both learn from experiences of others, as also contribute to the global experience in planning and implementing Information Technology projects.
- Government of India should consider participation in the Government On-line (GOL) Project originally launched in 1995 by ministers from the G-7 countries.
- A systematic exercise should be carried out by government departments for identifying those tasks that can be effectively done through telecommuting. An option can then be given to employees to accomplish their work through telecommuting.
- It is necessary to recognise the strategic nature of Information Technology in government and to ensure consistency, connectivity and inter-operability.
- Government of India should set-up a Central Repository of data elements in government. The Repository could perhaps be set-up with the National Informatics Centre. Each data element

should be owned by a single agency. The Revenue department in each state could own for example data on citizen name and address. Each agency should provide a comprehensive listing in the Central Repository of its captured data elements, and the platforms and databases where such data elements reside.

- The Survey of India should make available digitised base maps with a threshold scale, free of charge and free of copyright restrictions. This would stimulate the market for development of value added applications and create new products and services. Similarly, the National Remote Sensing Agency should also make available remote sensing data for easy access by the public.
- There is a distinct need to reorient the civil service for meeting the challenges of the future. Training can and must play an important role in improving the skills and quality of the civil service. Employees should be encouraged to make learning into a highly self-motivated activity for the acquisition of new knowledge and skills.
- The Information Age will present qualitative discontinuities and the typology of the civil service will witness a shift from the earlier command and control structure towards on characterised by staff empowerment and team working. There is also greater requirement for inter-disciplinary teams, as the task of administration becomes more complex.
- The Internet will be one of the most useful of mediums for managing and disseminating government information and consequently exclusive training will be necessary for setting up and maintaining websites.
- It is necessary to have staff with domain knowledge who can help architect systems that are practical and effective in delivery of services to citizens.

The National Task Force submitted its second background report on 8 August, 1998. The third Basic Background Report on Strategic Policies was submitted on 18 March, 1999. These recommendations constituted a paradigm shift from the earlier concepts and strategies adopted for growing IT industry in India. These reports sought to orient policies towards the creation of appropriate investment climate and streamlining the procedures for minimising uncertainty.

The Task Force, *inter alia*, identified Citizen-IT Interface as one of the key areas to service the information requirements of citizens through deeper penetration of IT in society and through the extensive use of latest tools in the networked society. It took note of the fact that while the government had been using computers for over three decades, in applications such as taxation, census, health, education, industry, trade, planning, etc. the information system had at best succeeded only in maintaining records in an effective way. It felt that the emerging network based technologies allow a fresh look at the Citizen-IT Interface. It observed that, in the systems hitherto implemented, the existing rules and procedures of the government were simply automated into computerised information systems. The existing computer based systems served bureaucratic interests and not people's interests.

The Working Group on Citizen-IT Interface recommended as follows:

- Government-wide electronic information infrastructure should be created to simplify service delivery, reduce duplication, and improve the level and speed of service to the public. This would provide the public (business and individuals) with the opportunity to send and receive, over electronic terminals, the information that currently passes between them and the government on paper.
- The government should encourage the establishment of Internet Service Providers (ISPs); this will provide access to the network based services from even the most remote locations in the country.
- The government and the private sector would need to collaborate to put in place Electronic Fund Transfer (EFT) system, since this is critical to the successful implementation

of Electronic Commerce, as well as direct service delivery to citizens.

- It is necessary that computers should be made cheaper to increase their penetration.
- Reengineering of the existing government processes and procedures is essential to bring about transparency in working, reducing bureaucratic controls, increasing efficiency and productivity, reducing cost of service delivery, etc. Integration of projects across various departments to provide a single point of contact for citizens for delivery of services electronically is essential.
- There should be complete transparency in governance. Citizen charter of each and every government department should be available to citizens over the Net.
- The Freedom of Information Act to be enacted which shall ensure right of citizen to have access to information.
- State Institutes of Public Administration should be reengineered to help bring about IT-Responsive State Governments. Alignment of IT and business requirements of government departments, and focus of citizen as a customer to deliver one-stop integrated services will be essential. The institutes should be reengineered to orient their thinking on the Citizen-IT Interface.
- A National Institute of Smart Government should be set-up to focus on all issues concerning IT-supported governance.
- Delivery of services should be on 'Transaction fee' basis. Private sector should be partner with government in electronic delivery of services. In view of the enormous capabilities of the private enterprises, they should be involved in public funded projects as far as possible.
- Service Delivery Points (SDPs) will have to be set up at convenient locations for citizens to access services. These will be established by the private sector. It specifically made mention of a few ideas to bring the service outlets closer to the people in all areas by the following means:

- Information Kiosks in public places such as shopping centres, post offices, railway stations, libraries, etc.
- PCOs upgraded to manned public access terminals. All the STD/ISD booths should be converted into IT booths through whatever necessary steps required to do the same. They will operate as Public Tele Info Centres (PTICs).
- Interactive Voice Response (IVR) Systems to be used as interface with databases for voice messages delivery to citizens.
- Front Office Terminals of Government offices.
- Domestic TV with a set-top box.
- Simple, easy to use, graphical user interfaces in local languages should be made available.

- Services should be delivered to citizens in Rural Areas in the following sectors:
  - Agricultural sector (Weather forecasting at the district level; price of commodities in major centres; availability of seeds and crop diseases etc.)
  - Education opportunities
  - Employment Exchange Registration
  - Public Grievances Registration and Tracking in written form

Urban Services

For citizens in urban areas, electronic billing and payment for the following utilities be introduced:

- Electricity Bills
- Telephone Bills
- Water Bills
- Property Tax Payments
- Road Tax

Smart Cards

In the long run, citizens must have unique identification cards. The usefulness of the card needs to be driven home by making it a multi-purpose card, which will help the citizen receive a number of benefits and services. A smart card citizen ID with multi-functions should be launched. The private sector should be actively associated by ensuring a business angle in the project.

For the full fruition of the ICT applications for governance, it was also suggested that Smart Cards, Stored-Value Cards, Credit/Debit Cards could be integrated in the framework of National Electronic Payment Systems for effecting payment of bills to utilities.

E-Procurement

Government tendering/procurement should be taken up as mission mode project. Electronic procurement and settlement system to eliminate the need for duplicate departmental systems. The following should be integrated:

- Suppliers' Database
- Procurement Database
- Financial Systems integrated with Payment Systems
- Electronic Catalogues for products and services for which contracts of business relationships exist
- Price, performance, delivery details, payment mechanism integrated into Catalogues to enable on-line decision making
- Transaction sets standardized

Tax Returns

The process of filing income tax return should be simplified and made electronic. A project in the area should be taken up with the active participation of the private sector.

Citizen Training

There is a strong HRD content in making the Citizen-IT Interface successful. Citizens at large have to be trained in addition to training the government officials in launching their respective systems.

- Citizens need to be trained in operating the user interface at SDPs. The mouse, touch-screens, keyboard, IVR, filling forms in regional languages.
- Government officials have to be trained in operating their databases, updating and maintaining them.

Citizen Information System

A few of the government departments should begin IT based information system straightaway to pave the way for practical IT Citizen Interface. Illustrative examples of such systems are given below:

- *Income Tax Information System*: Such a system should give full details of the IT-net latest Tax laws. Templates for calculation of Tax by the employees or simple business personnel should be available on-line. Any clarifications/ queries should also be addressed on-line. If not possible, then through E-mail.
- *Customs and Central Excise Information System* should be developed similarly and should give tariff schedule and how to meet Central Excise and Customs obligations and requirements, meet the procedures, etc. It should provide for query/clarification through E-mail.
- *Career Guidance System for Youth*: Such a system should have the following components:
  — *Electronic Employment Exchange*: It should be possible for youth to register themselves for jobs based on their qualifications, capabilities and interests.
  — *Career options* available in different areas including

options for higher studies in any professional area. Links should be provided to the Websites of different institutes/ organisations dealing with the subject.
- — Information of Small Savings policies, Bank Loan Schemes. Insurance Schemes, IRDP Loan Schemes and other investment plans.
- — Special schemes for scheduled castes and backward classes as a separate service so as to ensure adequate focus and easy dissemination of information.
- — Health Information System.

Motor Vehicle Licences

Driving licences (new and renewals), vehicle registrations, vehicle transfers, inspection of commercial vehicles and all other public dealing works under the Motor Vehicles Act could be handled by the respective State Governments.

Pilot Projects

Pilot projects should be taken up jointly by the Central and State Governments to demonstrate the feasibility and the usefulness of Information Technology. It is proposed that Government of India fund the following projects immediately:

- Project on Municipal Corporation (Water Tax), Transport (Railway Ticketing), Road Transport (Ticketing and Time Tables) and Education related project as specific IT Interface to be made available to citizens through the Internet ready booths in Chennai.
- Hospital Information Dissemination and Registration Project in Punjab.
- A similar project on Agricultural Prices Dissemination. The latter could in time be upgraded for use in trading. The information part could be used to create early warning for the government with respect to shortage, surplus and prices

of crops. Eventually, a full-fledged system based on crop prices could help both the government and the citizens.

- Collectorate services to citizens.

Working Group on IT for Masses

On the recommendations of this Task Force, Government of India initiated several regulatory and promotional measures to remove impediments and enable the growth of IT industry in the country and to enable large-scale applications of IT in various areas related to day-to-day lives of the people. Simultaneously, the government was conscious of the possibility that these developments could create a new division in society, referred to as *digital divide.* Government wanted to ensure that the benefits of Information Technology did not remain confined to higher classes of society and intended that IT be looked upon and used as a major instrument to provide new opportunities to those segments of society who did not see opportunities to improve their quality of life and had to reconcile to their fate. The belief was that if any technology could create new opportunities to bridge the gap between haves and have nots in society in the present times, it is Information Technology. With a view to giving a concrete shape to this thinking, it recommends 'catalytic, pro-active and enabling steps to be taken by the government to convert this commitment into an operational mechanism'. Government constituted a Working Group on Information Technology for Masses on May 10, 2000.

The terms of reference for this Task Force included, *inter alia*:

> *To recommend development schemes/programmes for citizen participation or taking IT to masses.*

The working group while making a brief mention of electronic governance observed as follows:

> "Government and its numerous agencies are the largest service providers in the country. It is obvious that in order

to have a visible impact of the benefit of IT on people, government must select major services at different levels such as Ministries/Departments of Central Government and State Governments, District Administrations, Municipal Services and services related to local governance at Block/Panchayat level, and re-engineer them through extensive use of IT. While over the years, there has been considerable progress in the use of IT in government services, most of these applications have been confined to back-office computerization. As a result, the improvement in quality of service to public has not made sufficient impact. It is, therefore, necessary that each one of the government agencies involved in providing citizen-oriented services should identify at least one area and use Information Technology in a highly intensive manner so that all aspects of delivery of service to people should transform into an IT based service. While doing so it would obviously be necessary that for sustainability of good quality of service to citizens, back-office component of the concerned agency for the identified application is fully computerised. However, the approach for computerisation and IT induction should be from front-office applications to back-office and not the other way. This will ensure that there is sufficient pressure on the government agencies from public to sustain the quality of service using IT. Back-office computerisation alone, which has very little impact on the public interface, is not sustainable in the long run due to lack of such public pressure."

Ninth Five Year Plan

The Ninth Five Year Plan did not mention 'E-government' or 'E-governance'. Stress was laid on the entire IT sector and the most important roadmap available was the one that was sketched out by the National Task Force. Following its recommendations, 1 per cent to 3 per cent of the budget of all the Ministries/Departments was earmarked for expenditure on IT applications. The Plan document expected this to lead to increased productivity in various sectors, timeliness of implementation of projects leading to the minimisation of time and cost overruns as well as creation of entirely new enterprises like software export, Internet-based enterprises, Electronic Commerce, etc. It visualized 'a propensity for IT-led development'. It also envisaged that the impact of IT will be especially predominant in the social sectors like health, education, judiciary and rural development.

In October 1999, the National Informatics Centre, which had pioneered the computerisation in government departments and other administrative agencies, was taken out of the Planning Commission where it was born and nurtured and together with the Department of Electronics, it constituted the new Department of Information Technology. The new department was to act as a nodal institution and facilitator in respect of all initiatives in Central and State Governments, academia, the private sector and successful Indian professionals abroad and "actively promote and accelerate the IT revolution in India".

The strategy followed during mid-nineties was to encourage the use of computers in the government and push more employees into the use of IT including the fast expanding Internet. In the process, some public services became improved although there was no big picture of how to go about it. Some notable successes were the railway reservation system and banking practices. Some states like Andhra Pradesh went in a big way in using IT and applications were put in place for drastically improving internal functioning of the government agencies.

Tenth Five Year Plan

The report of the Working Group on Convergence and E-governance took note of the fact that the picture of E-government or E-governance presents a wide variation of the level of computerisation and the use of IT enable applications within the government and for delivery of services and information. It also felt that though, a minimum agenda had been devised for computerisation of the governments, there was no real total picture of the country or any marking of the level up to which IT was being used by governments.

It defined the scope of E-governance and mentioned that it involves transformation from being a passive information and service provider to bringing active citizen involvement. Its dimensions could include the following:

- Single source of information for citizen
- Equality and ease of access
- Optimising resources of multiple organisations
- Intergovernmental participation
- Public networks
- Involving various stake-holders
- Stimulating debates
- Exchanging views and information
- Increasing participation by citizens in decision-making
- Public information feedback

It was suggested in the report that the Master-plan of E-governance should be guided by the following:

- A clearly focused vision of what is the objective of introducing E-governance.
- The range and standards of delivery of information and services to the people must be defined with time frames within which they are to be attained.
- Any plan or scheme for E-governance should have sustainability; it should not be a mere novelty at government expense only for the sake of doing something that is in fashion.
- Standardisation should be started without any delay otherwise confusion will ensue that would negate the advantages of use of IT.
- Areas of public funding should be clearly spelt out.
- The situation in various States should be gone into in details and appropriate plans and schemes suggested suited to different States.

- Interactivity must be built into all schemes of E-governance otherwise it will only remain as a labor saving device for the government functionaries.
- In the matter of E-governance, G2G, G2C, G2B functionalities have necessarily to be developed. E-governance is to be understood in the sense also of governance even of public and private corporate bodies, Municipal Corporations and even local bodies. If E-governance is to be ushered in an effective manner, it is necessary to create set of 'flash pictures' of the state of E-governance in the country.

The following schemes have been included in the plan:

(In crore rupees)

Computerisation of Secretariat	3 % of Plan
Creating India Portal (single window)	100
Development of Local language Tools and Content	50
Evolving IT Architecture (Guidelines, Best Practices, Standards and support for Pilot/Test-bed projects etc.)	50
Technical Support to State Governments for accelerating E-governance practices	50
Creating Citizens data bases through ID/Smart Cards	600
Research for Information Security, covering: • Technology for E-Commerce • Information Security, Encryption, Digital Signatures • Public Key Infrastructure • Smart Cards • Bio-metrics • Digital Rights Management	300
IT for Masses (Support for Multi-functional Community Information Centre)	700

The efforts of the State Governments were earlier guided, stimulated and coordinated by the NIC. However, as some states are becoming more and more IT savvy, many began conceiving and implementing their own programmes which did not have uniformity. The Tenth Plan has made provision for standardisation and it would be expected that utmost importance is given to this aspect. Similar is the case with the re-engineering of procedures. Although it finds mention in the Plan, this is the most difficult part of the exercise to bring about E-government which may lead to E-governance in the sense that it is understood and implemented in many parts of the world.

Four

Andhra Pradesh

Andhra Pradesh was the first State in the country to take up E-government in a systematic manner under a clear-cut vision backed up by a policy frame that not only supported the programmes for computerisation and single window delivery systems but where such efforts were initiated, monitored and facilitated by the Chief Minister of the state himself. It was in 1998 when its first e-governance project, called CARDS, was initiated as computerized property title registration and stamp duty payment service. The state moved extensively and fast in the march to E-governance and a number of services and information were made available on the net.

The six main projects that have laid the foundation of E-government in Andhra Pradesh are: APSWAN, CARD, TWIN, MPHS, APDMS, SKIMS and FAST. Each one of these was conceived with a clear vision about the benefits and advantages in terms of information or service to citizens and deployed IT capabilities towards this end. On another plane, the state gave unprecedented push to the IT industry and created conducive environment for it to grow at a fast rate.

IT Policy 2000

In July 2000 the Government of Andhra Pradesh initiated its Information Technology Policy 2000, arising out of its Vision 2020 document. The vision of the State for the IT sector was that *Andhra Pradesh will leverage Information Technology to attain a position of leadership and excellence in the information age and to transform itself into a knowledge society.* The objectives of the IT policy were:

To use IT as an instrument to foster the *economic development of the state.* This required specific action for:

- Growth of IT Industry in the state
- Growth of employment potential
- Attracting investment from outside the State
- Providing high quality of services in all spheres
- Providing knowledge as the key resource for economic programmes of individuals and institutions.

IT projects aimed at improving the internal efficiencies to benefit the poor also through better planning and targeting and through superior enforcement of law.

Together with economic development, an improved quality of life to the citizens has to be assured. These include the following:

- Quality, standards and universalisation of education
- Access to quality health care for all
- Availability and nutrious food for all
- Development and centers of excellence in knowledge.

Good Governance

With the growing realisation all over the world that Good Governance is necessary not only for the orderly functioning of the society but also for carrying out development and welfare measures effectively, the possibility that IT can significantly impact on the quality of governance was made an integral part of the policy. At the time when this process was initiated in Andhra Pradesh, the concept and practices of electronic governance were still taking shape in the global context. Very few models were available which could fit the Indian picture fully. Thus, it was broadly found necessary and possible to improve Government-Citizen interface, Government-Business interface and Infra-Governmental processes with the use of IT.

It was envisaged that IT shall be used not merely to automate processes but as a strategic tool to simplify procedures and revamp processes. Electronic governance would bring in the following benefits:

- Anywhere, any time services to citizens
- Better accountability, responsiveness and transparency
- Highly efficient government machinery and systems
- Reduced direction and arbitrariness

The IT policy 2000 was not meant to be a static document since the nature and pace of development of Information Technology required that such a policy frame should be dynamic and evolutionary which could take into its fold emerging technologies and trends. It was, therefore, proposed to update the policy as frequently as required.

ICT Policy 2002-2005

The ICT Policy that was initiated in 2002 augmented the functioning of the ICT sector to give it a new direction. The Policy was aimed at promoting growth of the ICT industry in the State and benefit the IT hardware and software industries, IT services, IT Enabled Services and the IT infrastructure industries. The government extended the policy to telecommunications companies, which included basic telecom service providers, VSAT, cellular companies, telecom infrastructure companies, and Internet Service Providers. To facilitate the overall growth of ICT industry in the State, the ICT Policy 2002-2005 aimed at creating an environment for realisaton of the Vision 2020 and adoption of Information Technology in all aspects of development including E-governance. This Policy gives a new direction to the ICT sector by providing thrust in the following key areas:

- *Preference to AP Units for E-governance Projects:* A weightage of upto 10 per cent in score to be given to IT units with registered offices in Andhra Pradesh, during the technical evaluation in all E-government projects.
- *Subsidy for SME's for participation in international events:* A 30 per cent subsidy would be provided to the SME units with turnover not exceeding Rs.10 crore in the preceding year in respect of the stall rent payable for participation in notified international events.
- *Promoting quality certification:* Reimbursement of 20 per cent of the cost on securing quality certification of Level 2 and above to promote quality consciousness and quality control among IT companies.

Some of the other incentives extended to IT companies in this Policy included:

- Exemption from purview of AP Pollution Control Act except in power generation sets
- Exemption from inspections under Factories Act, Maternity Benefit Act, AP Shops & Establishments Act, Contract Labour Act, Payment of Wages Act, Minimum Wages Act, Employment Exchanges Act
- Permission to run a three shift operation
- 25 per cent rebate in power tariff for a period of 3 years
- 50 per cent reimbursement of the stamp duty, transfer duty and registration fee
- Exemption from zoning regulations
- Rebate in cost of land
- Capital investment subsidy
- Special provision for IT projects with investment of Rs.50 crores and above

Free Right of Way

Creating the physical infrastructure for telecommunication by laying optical fibre cable is a basic real condition for the practicability of applications that require broad-band capacity. Arduous, confused and time consuming processes were involved in sorting out the issues of right of way involving a number of agencies that owned the land along which cabling had to be done. This could result in holding back the entire telecommunication and E-governance plan all over the country. Andhra Pradesh overcame this with a quick decision and became one of the first states to promote 'free right of way' for telecommunication purposes along highways. The process of cable laying was accelerated and the work was completed in record time.

E-Government Initiatives

Recognizing the need for technology-enabled service delivery and, as a part of its E-government strategy, the State government initiated an innovative broad based, enterprise-wide approach to service delivery. The targeted benefits of E-government programme include the following:

- Streamlined, standardised electronic information gathering and access
- Electronic delivery of services to meet citizen expectations and requirements
- Convenient, any time, anywhere citizen services
- Support for E-commerce initiatives (e.g., on-line filing, payments etc.)
- Significant improvement in Government to Citizen (G2C), and Government to Business (G2B) interfaces

ICT Architecture for E-government

The Government of Andhra Pradesh realised soon enough that computerisation and use of ICT in isolated islands would create more complications than good and that the government departments cannot follow 'stand alone' approach. Interoperability of the systems was most necessary which should be introduced from the very start. It realised that in order to implement and gain the advantages of E-government, the State must consider itself as one entity in which all parts work together for the common good by avoiding duplication of efforts and share technical assets. The State used the enterprise approach which made state-wide perspective as the basis for designs rather than technological perspective, thus attempting to synchronise multiple applications that run on a number of infrastructure components.

It was not easy to do everything in all departments simultaneously or to speed up beyond a point and some sort of prioritisation was necessary. A number of issues had to be sorted out which would determine as to which applications should be taken up first and which should wait. It was necessary to identify such applications which were in line with the global best practices. The answer to these questions was found through an exhaustive ground level survey of the governance practices within the major departments and agencies. Logical grouping of departments, based on comparable objectives was done and the core processes of the departments were mapped. Feasibility matrix for each group was worked out and the priorities as well as the phasing of introduction of the applications was thus determined through a highly scientific and professional process.

The Core Applications and projects that emerged were the following:

- *On Line Transaction Process (OLTP) System* to provide a single window to citizens to access the services across multiple departments and achieve horizontal and vertical integration of departments at Mandal, District and State levels—the focus was on data management system, integrated land management system and Geographical Information System. As on April 2002, pilot projects at Bhangir and Shadnagar Mandals involving 10 departments were taken up which were to be extended to others.
- *Electronic Services to Citizens (E-Seva)* under the Public Private Participation model—A number of services have already been rolled out as described below:
    - 35 E-Seva centres (with 280 service counters) have been set-up. spread over the Twin Cities of the capital and Ranga Reddy district.
    - There are no jurisdictional limits and any citizen in the

twin cities can avail of the services at any of the 35 E-Seva service centres.

— All service counters are facilitated with an electronic queuing system.

— The centres function as "One-stop-shop" for over 30 G2C and B2C services.

— Online services like E-forms, E-filing, E-payments by cash/cheque/DD/credit card/Internet are accepted.

- *Single Window for Business* to provide access to services across multiple departments under the PPP model-but it is yet to take off.
- *Social Benefits Management System* for monitoring and tracking various welfare schemes and better targeting of beneficiaries in the initial process.
- *Complaints redressed through help-desk and call centers* with centralized tracking the system is yet to take off (Sept. 2003).
- *Integrated Financial Information System:* For integration of applications in Finance department and its associated departments.
- *E-Procurement:* Applying E-government concepts and technologies to the area of government purchases to reduce prices of goods and services. There is scope for PPP model to be applied.
- *Human Resource Management System*: Centralised payroll and G2E portal enabling self-service zones for government employees numbering about one million.
- *Generic Office Management System (Smartgov)* involving workflow automation—a total of 483 applications across 30 departments been identified and were to be extended to the district level.
- *Government Portal:* a common gateway for all state services, applications and information. The Portal was launched in March 2002. Some more details about the Portal are mentioned later.
- *Secure Intranet:* The objective is to provide communication

infrastructure to connect all the locations of government offices. In a limited sense, this has been put in place by providing connectivity from the state capital to the district offices.

- *Data Centre:* A central facility where the application and database servers would be located and which would be the focal point for hosting all major applications and data of government departments.
- *Kiosks in rural areas:* To provide access points for rural locations. This was to be done under the Public-Private Participation model.
- *Public Key Infrastructure:* For enabling secure E-commerce to take place over internet through digital signatures. This was to be implemented under the PPP model.
- *Identity Cards for citizens:* Unique identification system for citizens based on comprehensive survey data.
- *Data warehousing:* To analyse the huge historic and archival data generated in the computerized departments and agencies. A project implemented jointly by the central and state governments did not yield desired result, therefore, it was decided to implement it on fresh lines.

ICT Architecture—The core actions include:

(a) Standards mandated through government orders
(b) Compilation of open technology standards
(c) A set of best practices in deployment of ICT
(d) Models to be improved incorporating a role for NGOs

Security Policy—Appropriate security policy and actions have been initiated.

Public-Private Participation for E-government—The E-government initiatives will be funded under the policy framework initiated in August 2001.

Changed Management Policy—The electronic governance paradigm requires changes in structures and framework. This is the most difficult part of the E-government transformation and is to be worked out with great care and caution.

Privacy Policy—Transparency in government actions has to be balanced appropriately against the privacy rights and interests of the stakeholders. This yet to be worked out at the time of writing.

Some of these initiatives were the continuation of earlier efforts while some were new. In some cases, e.g., Changed Management Policy, fundamental rearrangements will be necessary.

It would be worthwhile narrating some details about a few important projects of Andhra Pradesh which have created some impact.

Computer-aided Administration of Registration Department (CARD)

The pioneering attempt at modernizing the service delivery system of the government was made through a project with a catchy name CARD given to the comprehensive project of computerizing one of the oldest wings of the Government, that had intensive dealings with the public and the functioning of which was archaic with a lot of scope for harassment and illegal gratification. The project was originally conceived in August 1996 and implemented at two test sites in 1997. Judging the project by its initial success and the immense potential it has in transforming the concept of public service, the Government decided to replicate it all over the State. This first attempt at using IT for public service was a significant step in E-government scenario in the country.

In order to give legality to the documents registered through CARD, Act No. 16 of 1999 was enacted under which the following important provisions were made:

- In the Registration Act, 1908, as in force the State of Andhra Pradesh, in sub-section (2) of section 2, after the words "includes a portion of book", the words "and the information storage devices like floppy disk, hard disk, compact disk" have been added.
- In section 16 of the principal Act, for sub-section (1), the following have substituted the original provision, namely:

"The State Government shall provide for the office of every Registering Officer the books and also the information processing and storage devices like computer and scanners along with the software prescribed by the Inspector General, from time to time necessary for purpose of this Act".

- In section 61, after sub-section (1), the following proviso has been added:

  "Provided that the copying of the items referred to above may be done using electronic devices like scanner."
- In section 70-B, the following provisions have been made:

  "Notwithstanding any thing contained in this Act or any other Law for the time being in force, a copy of any document registered and scanned using the electronic devices and certified or attested by the Registering Officer in-charge of the office shall also be received in evidence of any transaction as is described in the said document."

Standards of Service

Most governments in the world who have effectively used IT in government, while embarking upon E-governance, have spelt out the standards of service that it would guarantee through citizen's charters. This has generally not been so in India where citizen's charters have only narrated the functions and responsibilities of the department or the agency. In Andhra Pradesh, however, it has been declared as a component of the service delivery system.

In the case of CARD, it proclaims:

> "We are committed to providing speedy, transparent and quality services to the registering public. We assure that our services will be accurate, reliable and timely."

It spells out in detail the actual timeframe guaranteed for responses and actions on various items by declaring:

We shall provide the following registration services measuring up to the standards mentioned below:

Service	Office Responsible	Time limit for delivery of service in offices covered by CARD Project	Time limit for delivery of service in offices not covered by CARD Project
(1)	(2)	(3)	(4)
I. STAMPS			
1. Sale of Stamp Paper	G.S.O., Hyderabad Sub-Registrar & E.O. Stamp Vendor.		
(a) upto 20 sheets		(a) 15-20 minutes	(a) 30-45 minutes
(b) 20-50 sheets		(b) 30-45 minutes	(b) 1 hour
2. Affixture of special adhesive stamps	G.S.O., Hyderabad Sub-Registrar & E.O. Stamp Vendor.		
(a) upto 50 documents (b) 50-100 documents			(a) 45 minutes (b) 1 hour & 30 minutes to 2 hours
3. Refund of value of stamps under the provisions of the Indian Stamp Act.	R.D.O in Districts. G.S.O., Hyderabad.	4 weeks	4 weeks.
II. REGISTRATION OF INSTRUMENTS			
1. Document writing on DMP/Laser Printer-without Plan & Annexures.	Sub-Registrar's Office		
(a) In the- prescribed format.		(a) 30 minutes/ one hour	(a) Service not available
(b) With extra clauses, for each additional page.		(b) 30 minutes extra	(b) Service not available
2. Issuing of Market value Assistance	Sub-Registrar's Office	10 minutes	10 minutes
3. Issuing Cash Receipt	Sub-Registrar's Office	10 minutes	5 minutes
4. Registration of instruments relating to sale, gift, partition, mortgage, exchange and lease.	Sub-Registrar's Office	1 hour without manual backup	3 days

(Contd.)

(Contd.)

(1)	(2)	(3)	(4)
5. Issuing certified copies of documents.	Sub-Registrar's Office	15-30 minutes 3 working days	3 days
(a) Documents registered through CARD system	Sub-Registrar's Office		
(b) Documents registered under manual system	Sub-Registrar's Office		
6. Making a reference to Collector u/s. 47-A of I.S. Act.	Sub-Registrar's Office	5 working days	5 working days
7. Registration of Societies and Firms	District Registrar	4 working days	4 working days
8. Representation on existence of anomalies in market value guidelines.	Anomalies Committee	8 weeks	8 weeks, within 2 weeks to the committee, 2 weeks for finalisation,2 weeks to commissioner, 2 weeks for final orders.
9. Deposit opening or withdrawal of sealed cover containing wills	District Registrar	3 hours	3 hours
10. Registration of Instruments not covered by item 4 above.	Sub-Registrar	3 days	3 days
11. Issue of Encumbrance Certificate	Sub-Registrar	20 minutes	5 days
12. MARRIAGES:			
Special Marriage	Sub-Registrar	2 hours on the day of appearance	2 hours on the day of appearance
Hindu Marriage	Sub-Registrar	After 30 days from filing of application Two hours—if the marriage is solemnized within five years preceding the date of application.	After 30 days from filing of application Two hours—if the marriage is solemnized within five years preceding the date of application.
Condonation of delay	District Registrar	10 days	10 days

How much of this is being followed on a sustained basis is, however, a matter of further field study which has not been covered in this work.

E-Seva

The success of the TWINS pilot project launched in Banjara Hills, Hyderabad, in December 1999 prompted the state to extend the experiment and provide services to citizens using state-of-the-art technologies. The project seeks to redefine citizen services by looking at 'service' from the citizens point of view, which is a new paradigm for governments steeped in the administrators point of view and convenience in everything where citizen-government interaction is involved.

Salient Features

- There are 35 'E-Seva' centres (with 280 service counters) spread over the Twin Cities and Ranga Reddy district.
- All service counters are facilitated with an electronic queuing system.
- The centres operate from 8.00 am to 8.00 pm, on all working days and 9.00 am to 3.00 pm on holidays, second Saturdays and Sundays.
- The centres function as 'One-stop-shop' for over 30 G2C and B2C services. There is no jurisdiction limits and any citizen in the twin cities can avail of the services at any of the 35 centres.
- On-line services are available for 'E-forms', 'E-filing', 'E-payments'.
- Payments by cash/cheque/DD/credit card/Internet.

Services for payment of utilities bills for the following are available:

- Electricity bills

- Water and sewerage bills
- Telephone bills (BSNL & TATA Tele Services)
- Property Tax
- Sales Tax

Other services include:

Certificates

- Registration of births/deaths
- Issue of birth/death certificates
- Registration Department: Issue of encumbrance certificates
- Issue of Caste/Nativity Certificates

Permits/Licences

- Medical and Health Department: Renewal of Drug Licences
- Issue/renewal of trade licences

Transport Department Services (available at Banjara Hills Centre only)

- Change of address of a vehicle owner
- Transfer of ownership of a vehicle
- Issue of learners' licences
- Issue/renewal of driving licences (non-transport vehicles)
- Registration of new vehicles

Information

- Transport Department Procedures
- Registration Department: Market value assistance

Reservation

- Reservation of APSRTC bus tickets
- HMWSSB: Reservation of water tanker
- Tourism: Reservation of tickets/accommodation

Other Services at 'E-seva' Centres

- Sale of passport application forms
- Receipt of passport applications
- Receipt of applications for new telephone connections
- Sale of non-judicial stamps
- Document writing service
- Collection of small savings

Internet Services

- Internet-enabled electronic payments
- Downloading of forms and Government Orders (GOs)
- Filing of applications on the web
- Receipt of complaints or requests in connection with citizen services

B2C Services

- ATM: Cash withdrawals and deposits
- ATM: Issue of statements of account
- Mutual Funds: Collection of applications
- Mutual Funds: Transfer of shares
- Cell phone bill payments

At the time of this compilation some of the planned B2C services were yet to take off.

Andhra Pradesh Portal

A rich and interactive portal has been launched by the state government which provides information and links to a large number of outside useful sites as well. It is a one point reference to a large number of information sources regarding facts, data and the services offered by various government agencies. By its very nature, it has to continue to evolve and it will take some time before it becomes fully functional. This is part of the online services of the government of Andhra Pradesh.

Andhra Pradesh Portal
Site Map

Home		
Government	Executive • Governor • Chief Minister • Council of Ministers • Secretariat Judiciary • Courts • High Court Judges • D.& S.J. Grade I Judges • D. & S.J. Grade II Judges	Legislature • Origin and Growth • Assembly Building • Legislative Committees • List of MLAs
About AP	A.P. Fact File • Spirit of AP • Agro Economy • Districts • Natural Advantages	History & Culture • History • Architecture • Arts & Crafts • Languages
Programmes/Schemes	Annapurna Scheme Deepam Scheme Food for Work Mathri & Sanhitha Programme	Antyodaya Scheme Dial your CM Janmabhoomi
Policies	Vision 2020 strategy papers Biotechnology Draft Budget	AP Budget 2003 Information Technology Industry & Commerce
E-Gazettes		
Discussion Forum		
News	Weather	
Sports	E-Cards	
Contact Government Elected Representatives Departments E-Citizen Lifecycle	Governor Cabinet	Chief Minister

The Web directory on this Portal lists and links the various public sector agencies involved in sectoral development and delivery of services.

Five

Gujarat

Gujarat started a little late the efforts to bring the benefits of ICT in governance. But it expressed a resolve to catch up fast. It had the benefit of the results and pitfalls of other models that were already on the implementation ladder. It did not follow the project-based approach of some other states but first conceived a long term scenario for the delivery of services and information to the citizens. It laid more stress on networking than computing power and application software.

IT Scenario in the State

At the end of November 2001, the IT scenario of the state was as follows:

STPI—registered IT companies	350
Software export revenues (crores Rs.)	70
ISP [licences issued]	110
International gateways	3
Internet connections	65,000
Estimated number of internet users	2,00,000

The IT Policy of Gujarat includes the mission "to help improve processes in the Government by using computing devices, communication systems associated electronics and software to provide better delivery systems to the citizens." The usage of IT strategies in Government is to aim at creating transparent government so as to fulfil the citizens charter. It does not aim at merely automating existing process but the target is to use IT to improve overall organizational efficiency and pass the benefits to the citizens of the State. The policy states that IT is not an end in itself but means to provide better quality of life to the citizens of the State.

Roadmap

The roadmap of E-governance envisages IT development in the State government through the following stages:

(a) For each department, identification of key areas on priority basis which need to be computerised first. The criterion would be computerising those systems first which improve the delivery systems for the citizens. This includes agencies handling ration card, driving license, sales tax return etc., in the first instance.

(b) By completing the data base in a time-bound fashion and making them operational. Delivery time for the citizens is to be cut down demonstrably in a time-bound fashion.

(c) Creating greater convenience for the citizens through efficient/intelligent interface which can take the form of computer-supported counters, kiosks etc. The Government would strive to ensure that all the forms required to be filled in by citizens for interface with the government are available for filling in electronically by the year 2005. Prior to this, citizens will have access to forms through kiosks and vendors by electronic devices. This had to be achieved by the year 2002 AD. The option of obtaining and completing forms by means other than electronic would be kept open.

In order to implement the programme it was essential to create an enabling mechanism. For this, all departments were asked to prepare their IT Action Plan, with one-year focus and a five-year perspective. One per cent of the State government's budget was committed to IT related activities which was expected to rise to three per cent in the year 2005 AD.

It was realized that effective training and orientation to bring about changes in attitudes of the government servants, whose productivity is sought to be improved, was important. Rigorous training on computer devices and the related hardware was considered necessary so that the fear of new technology was overcome.

For maximum productivity, simplification of procedures and large-scale delegation of powers was considered imperative. Tiered training programmes were conceived in which operating level personnel would be trained in the working of specific transaction system, middle level in handling of Management Information Systems (MIS) and senior level personnel to emerging trends in IT as rate of obsolescence of technology in this area is very high.

With a properly conceived roadmap being the destination structure, the implementation process started with the electronic linking of all the government departments. Simultaneously, stress was laid on ensuring computer presence in the villages. The creation of the information corridor, by linking the state capital and all the administrative centers down to the taluka level electronically, was given high priority.

Project Initiatives

Building on the available resources and taking into account the activities already taking shape the state initiated several projects to reach the governance process to the rual areas. Some of the important projects are described in the subsequent paragraphs.

Gujarat State Wide Area Network (GSWAN)

The Government of Gujarat gave the first priority of action to access and networking and made it the first item on agenda. It planned and implemented Sachivalaya Integrated Communication Network and

Gujarat State Wide Area Network (GSWAN) interconnecting all administration nodes at the capital city of Gandhinagar, Districts and Talukas. GSWAN, which was commissioned by the state government on 26 December, 2001 is an end-to-end IP based network designed with all services converging on to the same system with compatibility to link other existing networks in Government. The open architecture of the system offers effective utilization of bandwidth resource, access dropouts for public information centers. The design is supposed to ensure reliability of more than 99 per cent. The Integration of Secretariat Campus Area Network (SCAN) with GSWAN has induced mutual synergy in two networks. All government offices have facility to host and manage their websites locally as different from other models where often a centralised agency manages site hosting.

The network is also interfaced with the VSAT system at central control station (SC), enabling coverage of remote locations in the state which are not a part of designed network. It connects even the last and smallest administrative units in administrative hierarchy, into the network.

The network topology was conceived as a three-tier structure and design for GSWAN was based on hub-and-spoke approach. Out of three tiers the first tier, which is line hub, is the Secretariat Center (SC) at state capital, Gandhinagar, wherefrom the highest level offices of Government function in the state. Various departments and hundreds of subordinate offices located at the state capital are connected to SC horizontally through Secretariat Campus Area Network. All districts and Taluka offices are vertically connected with SC the hub of wide area network. The second tier constitutes District Centers, or DCs, located at district collector's office, and multiple district level offices are connected with DC horizontally. The third tier constitutes Talukas Centres, or TCs located at Taluka Mamlatdar's office and a few of the Taluka level offices are horizontally connected with TC. Each Taluka has a LAN port, FXS/FXO port and capacity to expand. All offices located at Taluka level are authorized to access GSWAN on dial-up lines in addition to direct LAN access. The systems provide flexibility to adapt to changing requirements of use and growth. The events taking place at remote locations are covered and connected to GSWAN through portable VSAT terminal. This has given tremendous flexibility to the state administration in reaching to the public in remote areas during any emergency.

GSWAN is an innovative and effective example of using converging technologies for E-governance and to matter the presence of states resources fell even in the remotest areas.

City Civic Centre—Ahmedabad Municipal Corporation

The Civic Centre has string of computers on the network and allows citizens to avail facilities like paying property tax, getting a death/birth certificates, file a water tap/drainage connection request, apply for building plan approval, lodge a complaint/grievance, make miscellaneous payments and everything which requires physical presence and can't be transacted on the net through website.

As the Civic Centre is on the network and connected to the main server which in turn is connected through the global internet protocol, the citizens can track the status of their application later on through the Corporation Web site. For doing so, a unique registration number is allotted to every applicant, which can be later used to track the status. The system also helps system managers and corporation management to carry out internal monitoring about the disposal and redressal of such applications putting paid to any chance of delay, harassment leading to nepotism and corruption. The operations of the City Civic Centre have also been connected to the web thereby bringing in transparency about the number of applications received and the concerned department to which they relate.

The following facilities are offered:

- Property Tax
- Vehicle Tax
- Building Plan
- Birth Application
- Death Application
- Shops

Collections through Civic Center (March, 2001)

Vehicle Tax	0601	881	5,01,009,50
	0602	123	75,029,50
	0603	1771	14,49,825,25
	0604	98	54,494,00
	0605	615	3,88,046,00
	0606	715	4,36,588,00
	0607	793	5,07,491,00
Sub-Total (7 Records)		**4996**	**34,12,483,25**

Source: Website

Mahiti Shakti—Citizen Service Portal

Based on the ideas and inputs from Collectorate of Panchmahals, Concept Centre for Electronic Governance (CCEG) of the Indian Institute of Management, Ahmedabad (IIM-A) in October 2000, developed a "proof of concept" portal for enabling Citizen to Government (C-G) and Government to Citizen (G-C) transactions using Information Technology as a medium. The "Proof of Concept" model of this project was launched on 4th October, 2001 across 14 Mahiti Shakti Kendras (MSKs). The initial idea was to study the response of this experiment and overcome the initial teething troubles and also enable the active involvement of the MSKs for getting valuable, practical suggestions and feedback to make this a viable, sustainable operation. The feedback was very encouraging and over 100 applications for setting up these MSKs at various locations were received.

NABARD also carried out a feasibility study and found an overall positive response to this activity based on which banks showed willingness to give finance to those MSKs that required loans. The initial "proof of concept" software which was developed by CCEG, Ahmedabad was later developed on a professional basis by an Internet solutions provider.

In order to give them a sense of involvement and to ensure sustainability, it has been decided to charge an empanelment fee of Rs. 8,000 from each Mahiti Shakti Kendra (kiosk). The amount collected from the information outlets has been put into a corpus fund, the interest from which sustains the day-to-day running of this project. It is proposed to have as many as about 100 kiosks initially.

Primarily, the project envisions a portal providing a single window to a full range of information and services. The project has been implemented with nearly 100 per cent Local Language interface using appropriate Internet technology. Along with the web application, an exhaustive GGIS package which provides information about more than 95 parameters like total number of schools, availability of water resources, etc. is provided. Along with the Mahiti Shakti Kendras, touch screen kiosks can be placed at appropriate locations for easy access by citizens.

The services that are available on this portal are:

(i) In respect of transactions of citizens with government, as many as 200 forms made available along with checklist giving details of documents to be attached with the form at the time of submission. For the district level offices, which have declared the citizen's charter, all the forms and checklists have been made available as a print-out at a prescribed fee. Details of the office to which each of these application forms are to be submitted are also indicated along with the time prescribed for the disposal of the application.

(ii) Information pertaining to ongoing schemes like those under the DRDA (District Rural Development Agency) and DPB (District Planning Board), TASP (Tribal Area Sub Plan) as also activities like scarcity etc. on parameters pertaining to each of these giving details like the name of the scheme, names of beneficiaries sanctioned in the last financial year, details of work undertaken, name of agency implementing the scheme and current status etc. have also been made available.

(iii) The web-enabled version of the Gujarat Geographic Information System (GGIS) developed by RESECO giving details of the resource availability in terms of 95 parameters of every village of the district is available on a query-based system.

(iv) Starting of electronic newsletter in the portal Mahiti Mahisagar featuring medical help, Legal help, Science corner, Children's corner etc.

(v) The Grievance Redressal Forum provides a forum for citizens to voice their specific complaints.

(vi) Electronic form submission for applications such as NOAPS (National Old Age Pension Scheme), Water related grievances and the Ration card application. The applicant fills the form at the kiosk. The processing is carried out by the staff and the final reply is sent to the applicant by e-mail and post.

(vii) Using these centers for the payment of utilities bills which would be tried out on a pilot basis.

(viii) Opinion poll on important issues pertaining to the public.

(ix) Chat with the Ministers and Senior officers of the district.

(x) Access to other important sites.

(xi) "Lok-Upyogi Mahiti" is a very important feature which provides useful information for citizens based on the experience, case studies and documentation of NGOs and other Agencies.

(a) Material on Irrigation from Development Support Center, an NGO specializing in that field.

(b) Material on Legal Literacy carefully prepared by the State Legal Aid Authority.

(c) Material in the local tribal dialect prepared by the BHASHA Sansthan on various features of the IPC, Cr.P.C. etc.

(d) List of over 1000 tested blood donors with details of their group, addresses and telephone numbers prepared by the initiative of LARA Foundation, Godhra.

(e) Useful information on over 30 specific crops grown in Panchmahals giving details of the seeds, fertilizers, insecticides, pesticides and organic manure etc. carefully and exclusively prepared for the portal by the GSFC (Gujarat State Fertilizer Corporation) Foundation.

(xii) Access to the electoral roll for anybody requiring the information for a useful purpose.

(xiii) Below Poverty Line list.

Tele Fariad (Public Grievance Redressal)

Making an innovative use of the GSWAN, Gujarat designed and commissioned "Chief Minister's Call Centre" or "Tele Fariad" for public grievances through the Network. Pilot for this scheme was started in Banaskantha District in December 2001. Experience was successful and another Call Centre was commissioned for Rajkot District in April 2002. The design consideration for the unique Tele-Fariad System included:

- A uniform telephone number for CM's Grievance Call Centre;
- Complainant should be able to deposit his complaint from anywhere in the State just by making a local call;
- Complaint should reach CM's office and processed same day; and
- The system should be cost effective to both Government and to the user.

Special four digit telephone number (1505) was allotted to be used throughout the State for Tele-Fariad System. Complaint deposited in original voice format is compressed and forwarded to designated mailboxes at CM's office, Gandhinagar to reach within 6-8 minutes. Voice messages are transcribed by the operators on a web based application developed by NIC, Gujarat and forwarded to related departmental head and others same day for necessary action under intimation to CM's office. Action taken on complaints is reconciled on receipt of replies from the department by the CM's grievance cell. People can inquire about the status of their complaint from the Collector's office or CM's grievance cell.

There were 2886 Tele-Fariads from Banaskantha District, till September 5th, 2002.

Employment and Training

The website for providing information and services relating to employment and training *www.talimroigar.org* is 'dedicated to all the Jobseekers of Gujarat State and also to the PROSPECTIVE EMPLOYERS.' It is a highly useful and user-friendly site through which any jobseeker can register, update or renew registration using the passwords, which may be obtained by clicking 'Password Request Form'. Establishments in Gujarat can obtain passwords from concerned Employment Exchanges or ITIs for using vacancy modules.

The portal lists a number of interactive services containing static and dynamic information. The following are clickable links to the information segments where further details can be accessed:

- List of Employment Exchanges/Offices
- Check your Registration Status
- Apply for New Registration at Exchange
- Update/Renew Existing Registration Card
- Know your Employment Status
- Information of Notified Vacancies
- Rojgar Samachar
- Career & Vocational Guidance
- Search Employers
- For Employers
- Search Employee from Exchange Data
- Submit EMI Returns
- Craftsman Training Scheme (CTS)
- List of ITIs
- List of Trades
- ITI Admission
- Admission Information Booklet 2002
- Seats to be filled for year 2002
- Application Status
- Apprentice Training Scheme (ATS)
- List of Apprentice Trades
- Apprentice Training Establishments

- Apprentice Vacancy Submission
- Exam Results
- For CTS Trainees and ATS Apprentices

The portal is full of information and details. Successive stages take the user down to details that are not generally made available or are thought as unnecessary for being posted for open viewing. The greatest advantage of making all these details available is that the information and processes are transparent which is the first positive consequence of E-governance.

As a test example, a segment was randomly selected for finding out the actual status and content. On clicking for Ahmedabad Employment Exchange, the following page appeared, which is reproduced as it was on 20 March 2003:

Ahmedabad Employment Exchange
Select qualification: Apprenticeship with ITI-522
View in Delhi

Name of Qualification	*Number of Candidates*	
Attendant Operator (Chemical Plant)	2	Detailed List
Auto Electrician	1	Detailed List
Auto Repairer	1	Detailed List
Book Binder	3	Detailed List
Computer Operator-cum-Programming Assistant	4	Detailed List
D.P.C.S.	7	Detailed List
Draughtsman Civil	2	Detailed List
Draughtsman Mechanic	6	Detailed List
Dress Making	1	Detailed List
Electrical Appliances Repairer	1	Detailed List
Electrician	70	Detailed List
Electronics Mechanic	29	Detailed List
Fashion Designer	1	Detailed List
Fitter	108	Detailed List
Instrument Mechanic	12	Detailed List

(Contd.)

(Contd.)

Name of Qualification	Number of Candidates	
Laboratory Assistance (Chemical Plant)	3	Detailed List
Lineman	10	Detailed List
Machinist	15	Detailed List
Machinist Grinder	2	Detailed List
Mechanic Diesel	22	Detailed List
Mechanic Maintenance (Chemical Plant)	1	Detailed List
Mechanic Motor Vehicle	82	Detailed List
Motor Vehicle Body Builder	3	Detailed List
Painter (General)	5	Detailed List
Plastic Processing Operator	1	Detailed List
Radio and Television Mechanic	1	Detailed List
Refrigeration and Air-condition Mechanic	25	Detailed List
Sheet Metal Work	6	Detailed List
Tailor (Men)	2	Detailed List
Tool and Dye Maker	3	Detailed List
Turner	28	Detailed List
Welder	23	Detailed List
Wireman	42	Detailed List
Total of Candidates	522	

On clicking on anyone trade, the *details* of the candidates with the following information appear in a tabular form:

Name Address Birth Date Caste Education Experience

Further detailed information can be seen on this portal about the seats, eligibility, list of establishments etc. pertaining to the Apprentice Training Scheme of the state. The concerned pages of the website as they appeared on 20 March, 2003 are reproduced below:

List of Apprentice Training Scheme (ATS) Trades

Sr. No.	Name	Duration	Eligibility	Type	List of Establishments	Seats Available	Seats Filled	Seats Filled By Company	Seats Vacant
1.	Advanced attendant operator (process)	18 Months	View	E	Establishments	0	0	0	0
2.	Apprentice food production (vegetarian)	24 Months	View	N	Establishments	162	0	0	161
3.	Apprentice food production (general)	36 Months	View	N	Establishments	124	11	0	112
4.	Attendant operator (chemical plant)	36 Months	View	E	Establishments	1135	330	0	826
5.	Attendant operator (dairy)	36 Months	View	E	Establishments	105	103	0	28
6.	Auto electrician	24 Months	View	E	Establishments	172	77	0	110
7.	Auto mechanic (two wheeler/three wheeler)	24 Months	View	E	Establishments	150	23	0	129
8.	Baker & confectioner	24 Months	View	N	Establishments	11	0	0	11
>>	>>	>>	>>	>>	>>	>>	>>	>>	>>
>>	>>	>>	>>	>>	>>	>>	>>	>>	>>
151	Winder (armature)	36 Months	View	E	Establishments	37	6	0	31
152	Winder (textile)	6 Months	View	E	Establishments	112	23	0	101
153	Wireman	36 Months	View	E	Establishments	861	251	0	656
Total						**28104**	**9616**	**6**	**19789**

Since this is only an illustrative exercise, all the rows have not been shown.

* E = Engineering * N = Non-Engineering

The next level of further detailed information regarding the establishments who offer apprenticeship and training under the specific trades is also available by clicking 'Establishment'. A randomly selected result is reproduced below (As it appeared on 20-3-2003)

Baker

List of Establishment(s)

Sr. No.	Name	Contact Person	ADDRESS	Seats Available	Seats Filled	Seats Filled By Company	Seats Vacant	Students	Status
1.	Modern Bakery India Pvt. Ltd.		G.I.D.C. Indo Estate Naroda, Ahmedabad Pin:382330 Phone: 0	1	0	–	1	View	Close
2.	Mahendra Mills Ltd.	G.D. Mevada	At-Kalol Dist. Gandhinagar Phone: 85541	3	0	–	3	View	Working
3.	Sweety Industries	Shri Rameshbhai D. Panjabi	44-45 GIDC Nadiad. Ta. Nadiad. Dist. Kheda. Pin-387 Phone: 66256	6	0	–	6	View	Sick
4.	J.P. Biscuit Bakery	Shri M.M. Kanjvani	96/97. Rangil Dasva, A.K. Road, Surat Phone: 44461	1	0	–	1	View	Close
	Total			11	0	–	11		

The usefulness of such a site or portal lies in its being updated regularly so that latest reliable information is available to the users.

Six

Karnataka

Bangalore, the capital city of the State of Karnataka came to be associated with IT right from its early stages of development. Karnataka established Electronic City way back in 1985, which provided entrepreneurs with land, water, incubation centre and excellent communication facilities. It was the first city in India where a satellite earth station was set up for high speed communication services to facilitate software exports. Well known companies like Infosys had their headquarters in this area.

The reasons why a large number of IT companies continue to chose Bangalore for location of their offices and operations is the ready availability of world class IT infrastructure and ample supply of specialised technical manpower. In addition it possesses pleasant and comfortable climatic conditions with cosmopolitan environment in the city along with a number of quality research and development institutions.

Software Technology Parks of Karnataka, a registered society, has played an important role in placing Bangalore and India on the IT map and has greatly helped in the IT development process across the state of Karnataka A Software Technology Park (STPI) was set up in 1991, which began by servicing 13 companies. The present number of companies being serviced is around 900. In 1999, STPI established earth stations in Mysore and Manipal.

It may be interesting to take a look at the milestones in the process of evolution of the IT industry in Bangalore:

- 1984-Texas Instruments enters India for offshore development.
- 1986-DoE announces software policy.
- 1991-Software Technology Parks of India (STPI) is set-up
- 1992-Exclusive satellite international gateway for export industry is set-up.
- 1997-Govt. of Karnataka announces IT Policy and Karnataka becomes the first State in India to do so.
- 1998-Number of IT companies under STPI grows to 253, with total projects worth US $840 million.
- 1999-Indian Institute of Information Technology, Bangalore (IIITB) and the KITVEN FUND are established.
- 2000-Number of IT companies under STPI grows to 782, with total projects worth US$1.1 billion.
- 2001-Number of IT companies under STPI grows to 928, with total projects worth US $1.58 billion.
- 2001-Number of hardware companies under EHTP grows to 24, with hardware exports worth US $0.076 billion.
- 2002-Number of IT (software) companies under STPI grows to 1038, with total projects worth US $2.06 billion (as of May 2002).
- 2002-Number of hardware companies under EHTP grows to 27, with hardware exports worth US $0.17 billion (as of May 2002).

Given below is an overview of the industry's composition during the years 1999-2002, in terms of the value in US dollars:

Value of Companies in US $ Millions	*Number 1999-2000*	*Number 2000-01*	*Number 2001-02*
Above US $200M	Nil	2	2
Between US $20M—200M	6	13	95
Between US S2M—20M	51	66	95
Less than US $2M	100	189	246
Less than US $0.5M	277	212	326

Source: http://www.bangaloreit.com/html/itsekar/itindustriesothercities.htm

Other IT Growth Centres in Karnataka

The State is concentrating on developing three more places as IT growth centres, namely Mysore, Manipal and Hubli. Mysore today is where Bangalore was 25 years ago, showing signs of being able to handle all changes that take place in a big city. The city has an abundance of technical manpower and its moderate climate makes it an attractive destination. It is well connected with Bangalore, just about 137 km away. The cost of living including land and housing is relatively low. The STP in Mysore was inaugurated in November 1998. A gateway satellite earth station was commissioned at the STP and operations were started in March 1999.

Manipal, situated in the Udupi district, and known for technical and medical education, is 65 km away from Mangalore and is well connected by road, rail and air. STPI Manipal started operations in November 1999 with the main objective of encouraging and promoting software exports.

Hubli, located in Dharwad district has a favourable climate and is well connected by road, rail and air services from Bangalore. The Software Technology Park in Hubli is housed in a 6-storied building and offers all facilities and services. The presence of IT in different places stimulates its use in different areas of application also and ultimately has an impact on the governance process.

Use of IT in Government and Computerisation

The Karnataka Government Computer Centre, which was established in 1971, was also one of the earliest to be set-up in the country. Use of computers was introduced progressively in the government but much was still to be done. During the last few years, almost as a sudden spurt in activity, a lot has been sought to be done in the field of computerisation and use of IT in the government.

From a report of the Department of Information Technology and Bio-Technology, the position obtaining in some important departments is quoted below indicating the progress of use of IT in government:

Secretariat LAN

- 1500 LAN nodes set-up in Karnataka Government Secretariat located in Vidhana Soudha, MS Building and New MS Building;
- The buildings are connected by Optic Fiber Cable;
- All section officers and above have been provided with computer systems and training has been imparted;
- Five applications—File Monitoring System, Letter Monitoring System, Personal Information Monitoring System, Budget Proposal Monitoring System and Court Case Monitoring System—are deployed on LAN;
- NICSI has deputed 8 programmers to assist in the function of the Secretariat LAN; and
- Chief Secretary's Office, Animal Husbandry & Fisheries, Forest, RDPR, Revenue, Urban Development and Kannada and Culture departments have implemented softwares developed by NIC.

CM's Secretariat

Information requirements of the Chief Minister's office are catered by project Mukhya Vahini in the following areas:

- Petitions Monitoring System (PEP) including follow up action taken on CM's instructions (ATR);
- Chief Minister's Relief Fund Management (CMRF);
- Action taken on Budget announcements (BUD);
- CM's Constituency Management System (CMS);
- Pending Papers with GOI (GOI);
- Issues of Districts (DIST);
- Departmental Information System (DIS);
- Private Sector Mega-projects Monitoring (GIM);
- Cabinet Section Computerisation (CAB); and
- Media Office Management (MED).

Agriculture Department

- Local Area Network established in the directorate;
- Database of 12,000 employees;
- Crop statistics from 1980-1997;
- Farm Management and Fertilizer Management System;
- Computerisation of about 100 RSKs (Raitha Samparka Kendras);
- FAQs, contingent crop plan available on the website;
- Major events such as NAME (National Agricultural Machineries Exhibition), Maize Mela etc. available on the website;
- Weather reports on daily basis; and
- Tips for farmers are available on daily basis on the website.

Website: http://raithamitra.kar.nic.in

Commercial Tax Department

- Payment of taxes, filing of returns, dealers registration, vigilance and intelligence activities computerised;
- Phase I and II—more than 1.5 lakhs records of 8 divisions computerised;
- More than 1 lakh dealer database being monitored;
- Computerisation in 9 check posts; and
- Phase III—computerisation of remaining 5 divisions awaiting government decision.

Website: http://kar.nic.in/ctax

Education Department

- CET-allotment of seats for professional courses computerised;
- CPl-SSLC and PUC examination processing computerised and the results are available on the web;
- Admissions for TCH and B.Ed. courses can take place on-line;

- Recruitment and transfer of teachers can take place on-line; and
- Placement of newly recruited teachers and probationary head masters are facilitated through computerised counseling.

Finance Department

- Computerised payment of taxes, filing of returns, dealers registration, vigilance and intelligence activities;
- Computerised Budget Information System (BIS) since 1992, which is available on the website http://www.kar.nic.in/statebudget;
- Public Works Finance Cell and ZP Unit computerised for monitoring monthly grants and releases.

Forest Department

- Software on financial accounting, forest offence cases, land use data, afforestation and wild life management has been developed and implemented on a pilot basis in Bangalore Rural Division;
- Computerised Range Management Information System (CORMIS) developed; and
- GIS Package developed and implemented for Hassan Division and Western Ghat projects.

Police

- Crime Criminal Information System (CCIS) software of National Crime Records Bureau (NCRB) is implemented in all the Districts and Police Commissionerates;
- About 1070 computers have been provided to various police units, out of which 549 stations (100 per cent in Bangalore City) have been equipped with computers;
- Third phase of Police IT 2000 project is in progress. The remaining 244 police stations will be provided with computers in this phase;

- In collaboration with NCRB, a major vehicle verification counter has been launched on 2 April, 2002, as a service to general public. It is becoming popular with the citizens; and
- Computers are being used for portraits building for identification of criminals, payroll, crime review statistics, personnel information system, *modus operandi* and for office automation.

Insurance Department

- Computerisation of motor vehicle branch is complete, providing details of more than 75,000 vehicles for insurance purposes. Details of more than 30,000 vehicles available; and
- Computerisation of the Bangalore and Mysore divisions (official branches) completed.

Transport Department

- Issue of driving licence with photo in Bangalore city;
- Computerisation implemented in five regional transport offices of Bangalore city and transport commissioners office, Bangalore;
- Computerised learner's licence, PVC driving licence, registration certificate, tax cards, tax/fee challans are being issued;
- Data entry for 2.5 lakhs vehicles completed;
- Computerisation of RTOs in Gulbarga, Mangalore, Mysore, Mandya and Dharward taken up; and
- Information kiosk installed in Yeshavanthpur RTO.

Website: http://rto.kar.nic.in

Municipal Administration

- Poura Vahini Project launched with a vision to computerise all the vital, basic and fundamental data;

- Details of pension liabilities in computer in the proforma prescribed by the World Bank; and
- Computerisation of service particulars of all the permanent employees of all the CMCs / TMCs and TPs coming under DMA completed.

Web site: http://www.worldwatch.org/bda

Water Resources Department

- Database for 30,000 tanks are computerised;
- Database for Hydro meteorological parameters are created; and
- Geometric centre is established for GIS, GPS and remote sensing applications.

Website: http://www.waterresources.kar.nic.in

Bangalore Development Authority

- Computerised allotment of alternate sites;
- Regular site allotment through internet; and
- Layout plans available using GIS package.

Kannada in Computers

- Common key board layout evolved;
- The formats and codes for Kannada Software standardised; and
- According to the set standards, software vendors have developed products.

Other Important E-governance Initiatives

Mahithi the Millennium IT Policy for the Common Man

The government of Karnataka announced the Millennium IT policy in order to *'refocus'* and *"define it in a way that is most suited for the present".* One of the objectives of the policy is to *"use E-governance as a tool and deliver a government that is more proactive and responsive to its citizens".* It also aims at promoting the usage of Kannada in Information Technology.

Taking note of the fact that computers are used in several departments and that statistical progress has been achieved in several departments in a decentralized manner, the Government has established a Centre for E-governance under the Department of Information Technology. This Centre will facilitate the use of Information Technology for the common man rapidly and effectively. It will provide technical support and coordination to all the Government departments in their IT projects and will also undertake a few critical projects that are likely to be used in more than one department.

Bhoomi Project

The project aimed at digitising rural land revenue record which is a crucial document in the lives of people. Such record is essential for security of loans, bail applications, getting scholarships for children, getting the benefit of rural development programmes, etc. Nearly twenty million land records containing details such as ownership, area, crop, bank loans, irrigation etc., covering 67 lakh farmers spread over 27,000 villages, were kept in manual format. Nearly 9,000 village accountants were maintaining these records and, the system was plagued with corruption, tampering of documents, non-availability of records in time, non-updation of records and non-availability of instant data for planning purposes.

The Bhoomi Project changed the entire system by converting the data into digital format. The information was made available to the people under a simple and user friendly procedure which was convenient and quick and became quite popular. In 177 talukas touch-screen kiosks were set-up from where farmers could get the revenue document within a short time by paying Rs 15 as user fee.

The process of degitisation, training and putting the scheme into operation involved about 20,000 man-months of data entry task followed by validation of nearly 20 million print-outs. These print-outs were distributed to 6.7 million farmers for their feedback. A large number of officials at the level of village accountants and deputy tehsildar were thoroughly trained for 177 sub-districts. The software for this was developed by the National Informatics Centre.

Nondani

The project is aimed at making land registration simple and easy for the citizens. People go to the sub-registrar's offices for registering sale deed, mortgage deed, etc., as well as for encumbrance certificate. This process requires a lot of manual operation and is extremely cumbersome. To simplify the procedures for citizens, the government initiated computerisation of the department. The sub-registrar offices in Shivaji Nagar, Kengeri and Bangalore South have facilities to scan the registration deeds and return the registered documents. So far, over 100,000 documents have been registered in a computerised environment. For giving the encumbrance certificate 13 year data needs to be incorporated into the computer. This process has been taken up. This will give relief to Bangalore citizens.

Khajane

This involves intensive computerisation of the treasuries all over Karnataka. The treasury payment system handles over Rs.20,000 crores annually through 225 treasuries. This system serves 4.7 lakh pensioners of government service, art and culture, sportsmen, journalists, freedom fighters, etc. In addition, the system serves 13.15 lakh old age pensioners, the physically handicapped and destitute widows. The treasuries act as bankers to 4.500 Zilla Panchayats, Taluk Panchayats, Grama Panchayats, Municipal Corporations and other funds. A comprehensive computerisation is planned using the V-Sat terminals. There will be a main data base centre at Bangalore and a disaster recovery centre at Dharwad.

Therige

Commercial Taxes Department has already computerised several facets of its operations. The details of about one lakh dealers are computerised by the department. In addition, important check posts are being computerised where the invoices will be scanned and the details of the transactions will be made available to the assessing officers to check evasion of taxes on certain commodities.

Karnataka Government Insurance Department (KGID)

Karnataka has the oldest insurance department started in the year 1891. It undertakes life insurance as well as vehicle insurance for its employees. The department offer life insurance policies for the employees as well as third party and comprehensive insurance for the vehicles. The motor branch of the department that offers insurance for vehicles is completely computerised. The computerisation of life insurance business is under progress.

Reshme

The State has introduced on-line transactions in the silk market. The cocoons are brought to the market, displayed and the trades are recorded online. This system has brought a lot of transparency in market operations.

Seven

Mizoram

Mizoram is one of the smallest States of the country which used to be only a district of the erstwhile Assam till 1972. It has the distinction of transiting from a State of armed insurgency to a land of absolute peace marching towards development in a determined fashion. It has the second highest literacy rate in the country and a forward looking people. With improved communication and connectivity, it shows promise in several sectors including IT and e-governance.

Realising the importance of IT, the government had taken first initiatives in 1991 with the establishment of an Electronics Cell in the Directorate of Industries and the Zoram Electronics Development Corporation Limited (ZENICS). However, the actual progress was confined to conducting training courses and nothing much happened in the field of E-government. The recent awareness created at the success of E-governance in the States of south India have inspired the governments in the far flung corners of the north east and a positive hope is visible. In the words of Shri K. Thangzuala, Minister for Industries and IT:

> *"We offer English speaking innovative people with a creative bent of mind that is needed for a dynamic industry such as IT."*

Due to very limited capacity of the State to fund its development programmes out of its own resources, the State has necessarily to depend on assistance from the Central Government. A number of project proposals were sent for approval and funding. The main projects are listed below:

Government of Mizoram Internet Backbone (GoMIB)

National Informatics Centre (NIC) is providing Computer and Communication based support to the State Governments through its satellite based computer communication network called NICNET. Since, there is a limitation in the NIC infrastructure, they cannot provide Internet connection to all the government offices. However, this can be overcome by strengthening NIC Infrastructure with state-of-the-art computer communication infrastructure for which the Government of Mizoram may provide all the additional infrastructure like Web Server, DNS Server, Mail Server, Proxy Server, Remote Access Server, PSTN line at least 30 connections, Dial-up Modem and Routers.

The objectives of the Internet backbone connectivity for the Government of Mizoram are:

(a) To provide Internet connectivity to all the government offices, undertakings, Public Information Kiosks, Citizen facilitation Centre/Kiosks;

(b) To provide transaction mechanism between various departments of the Government of Mizoram and their subordinate offices located at remote areas so that a substantial part of transfer of files and paper can be replaced by an Internet within the government.

(c) To incorporate E-mail facilities into the normal ways of contact methods for all the Government employees.

(d) To provide websites for all Government departments so that the common people can also see the progress of all the departments through CICs.

Secretariat Campus Area Networks

The Government of Mizoram was planning to IT-enable all the Secretariat offices for increasing quality services, reducing costs and improving overall efficiency and effectiveness in the Government. To achieve this, it was intended to network the entire secretariat complex using fiber optic cable and ATM switching technology. The proposed secretariat campus area network solution can be divided into three parts and implemented accordingly:

Part I: Cabling Infrastructure
Part II: Networking Infrastructure
Part III: Internet Connectivity Infrastructure

IT Learning Centre at Secretariat Complex

The centre would provide institutional training facilities by conducting in-service training programmes for officers and staff of State government departments including State civil service officers. The institute will provide hands-on training on various application software along with latest trends in Information Technology. *The Government of Mizoram intend that IT literacy be made compulsory for recruitment to the government services.* All the existing staff of the government departments are expected to attain IT literacy in the five years.

IT Entrepreneurs Development Programme for Educated Unemployed Youths of Mizoram

The aim of this project is to uplift the skill and capacity of educated unemployed youth including unemployed engineers and graduates for sustainable self-employment generation through IT entrepreneurship development programme. It would have the following specific action objectives:

- To provide special training to BE (Electronics and Communication) and BE computers in advanced software development environments so that they can be competitive in the world market.
- To provide a right mix of application exposure in the

domestic computerisation using the latest software technology through the nodal department.

- To develop a pool of trained manpower in Mizoram which may directly or indirectly help the growth of software industry in the State of Mizoram.
- To send about 20 students out of the 200 students to neighbouring countries either as faculty in IT or to work in information technology area.
- To produce entrepreneurs by training them in IT related subjects and project management whereby they are capable of opening IT training centres on their own with or without government assistance to further train more and more Mizos with an ultimate aim of making all Mizos IT savvy.
- To assist the youth of Mizoram by training them in IT related subjects with a view to producing trained faculties to impart further training in the State of Mizoram both through private IT institutes and through government sector by training all government employees.
- To produce trained manpower to undertake software development jobs both for the state of Mizoram and for the global market.

E-Governance Plan

The Government of Mizoram has taken cue from the approach followed by the Central Government for bring in E-governance to the departments and also taken ideas from the success stories in other states. The size and population of the State being very small, it is ideally suited for SMART governance, which, in expanded terms, means, improving services to citizens and business by providing Simple, Moral, Accountable, Responsive and Transparent (SMART) governance.

The Government of Mizoram foresees that services to citizens will be made available through various delivery channels (department interfaces, integrated citizen interface counter, internet, information kiosks, etc.). Some key benefits that can be achieved through E-governance are:

- Improved quality of service to citizens
- Improved efficiencies within the Government
- Better enforcement of law
- Education and information dissemination

The broad objectives that drive the conceptualisation of projects E-governance are:

- Enabling Government of Mizoram to provide better service and responsive administration tuned to the needs of the people.
- A knowledge driven society.

For achieving these broad objectives, the immediate actions and objectives were conceived as follows:

- Internet/Intranet Connectivity—Interconnecting all Government Departments, all District and RD Blocks Headquarters and Public Information Kiosks.
- Development of a number of Web enabled applications, electronics document processing, inter-office communication and document interchange.
- Maintaining elaborate data banks of citizens, departmental schemes, programmes, policies and procedures.
- Training and capacity building for all the government employees and creating awareness programmes among citizens.

Mizoram Portal

Mizoram Government sees its proposed Portal as a large website containing huge amount of Mizoram Database in the form of graphics, animations, texts, pictures, etc. empowered with Search Engine, linking to other sites, and Mail Server. Its objective would be:

- To presenct website containing all the departmental works and projects.
- To deliver government information relevant to public at large.
- To market agri-produces, handloom and handicraft products, passion fruits products, etc.
- To promote tourism industry in Mizoram.
- To promote Mizo cultural heritage.

Multimedia Content Creation Centre at ZENICS

In order to encourage creativity and use it to provide self-employment to educated unemployed persons in Mizoram through vocation of content creation fuelling entrepreneurship and widespread effective education and training on rural, social and economic upliftment topics, a Multimedia Content Creation Centre has been proposed. It would help in imparting professional training in Multimedia content creation to persons who may impart further training at their institutions and act as producer/entrepreneur or themselves take employment in content creation industry.

It would help in private setting up of information kiosks in public places for easy access to government information, procedures and policies.

Community Information Centre (CIC)

In 1999, the Ministry of Information Technology (MIT), Government of India mooted the concept of Computer Centres at every block of the seven north eastern states of India, including Sikkim, to be linked to a central server for information exchange and sharing, Internet facility and E-mail. This was a novel idea, as for the first time in the country a large network of this nature and magnitude was planned. This project was known as the *Community Information Centre (CIC) project.* Under this scheme, hardware and software were to be procured and installed under the aegis of the MIT. Each of the development blocks and districts headquarters were to be equipped with computers in a Local Area Network (LAN) and linked with

V-SAT to a central facility at New Delhi. With the help of these Centres, public will be able to access Internet at block level and district level and they will also be able to exchange information through E-mail, Chat, and File Transfer Protocol (FTP).

IT Education in Schools

With a great enthusiasm and attraction for IT and IT enabled services and vocations, the State has tried to universalise the knowledge of computers and IT by introducing it as a compulsory subject from the level of Class-III to Class-VIII and elective subject from the level of Class-IX to Class-XII. This project proposal on "Computer Education Plan for the State of Mizoram" was submitted to the Ministry of Human Resource Development, Government of India which has provided ten computer systems per school for 40 schools in Mizoram during the financial year 2001-02.

With these initiatives having been taken to coneptualise, projectise and pose these for funding to the Central Government, the ball seems to be in the centre's court. The Government of India would do well by realizing that with a number of advantages like compactness of areas and the homogeneous nature of the population with strong motivation and knowledge of Roman (English) script, the State can very well be turned into a smart state where the model of E-governance, which means going beyond delivery of services and information, can be introduced and an element of interactivity and participation of people can be procured as is happening in some advanced countries with high level of E-governance in place.

Eight

Uttar Pradesh

The vision stated in the IT policy of 1999 of the State is: *To use IT as a vehicle for economic development and to create a high-tech society with a high quality of life in Uttar Pradesh.*

The State did not flow in the first flush of IT wave but the presence of industrial towns like Kanpur, several institutions in state like the IIT, Banaras Hindu University, several well known engineering institutions, the HBTI and many central and state research laboratories gave it the necessary background and basic capability to develop information technology industry, training and education as well as applications. The unique location of NOIDA, almost as a part of Delhi, was also an asset waiting to be exploited. The State, therefore, intended to 'harness the advantages' and *'to place it on the global map of IT as the new Silicon Valley of India'.*

The stated objectives included:

- Accelerated development of Information Technology industry in the State and increase in both domestic and export earning in the software and hardware sector in IT;
- To create a SMART Government that uses IT for speedy, transparent accountable and efficient conduct of the government systems and services;
- To encourage and accelerate the use of Information Technology in schools, colleges and educational institutions

in the State, to enable the youth of the State to acquire necessary skills and knowledge of IT, thereby making them highly employable, the IT sector will be developed in order to provide increased employment opportunities.

- To bring IT within the easy reach of the common man and to make it useful to his daily need.

IT in Government

There was no overt use of term 'E-governance' or 'E-government', yet the vision was to make U.P. a 'Smart State' in 10 years in so as far as IT application in Government was concerned. The strategy and the roadmap was worked out with several important actions envisaged, some of which required not only detailed planning and working out of further execution strategy but also selection of best option and concerted efforts on the part of more than one agency or department of the government. The following targets and actions were envisaged:

- Training of all government employees in use of IT and its products over a period of 5 years.
- Linking of all government offices upto district level by the year 2000, upto tehsil level by 2001 and block level by 2004 with the help of suitable funding mechanism to be finalised with national/international funding agencies.
- Developing NOIDA/Greater NOIDA, Ghaziabad and Lucknow as Smart Cities by the year 2000, Gorakhpur, Kanpur, Aligarh, Bareilly and Agra by the year 2002. Allahabad, Moradabad and Varanasi will be developed into smart cities by the year 2003, rest of the divisional headquarters by 2005 and the remaining State by the year 2008.
- World class G.I.S. solutions in the fields of land record management, watershed management, master plan preparation, revenue collection, registration of documents, tourism facility management, agricultural input

management, hospital and health management. State Plan preparation, law and order administration, etc.
- Promotions and crossing of efficiency bars of government officials will be linked to computer literacy.
- All tax collection activities will be computerised in two years.
- The State Government will earmarked one per cent of the departmental budgets for computation and training of personnel.

In order to overcome the problems that could result in slowing down the pace of extending the connectivity and as a part of the overall strategy to lay proper infrastructure, facilitating the process of spreading connectivity quickly and creating trained manpower, the State created the following legislative provisions:

- U.P. Public Land (Optical Fibre Cable Laying and Maintenance) Act, 2001.
- Maharishi University of Information Technology Ordinance, 2001.
- Jagadguru Rambhadracharya (IT) University Ordinance, 2001.
- Amity Technology University Ordinance, 2001.

Following the pattern spelt out by the Central Government, the other enabling and resource issues were addressed by the following:

- Allocation of 2 to 3 per cent of annual Budget for IT with a system of monitoring the allocation for each Department.
- Department with direct interface with the public taken up for computerisation on a priority basis.
- An intranet for ensuring smoother flow of data, communications and access to information by different Ministries and Departments.
- Websites for Departments.

Availability of Computers

It was realized that the introduction of computers in every Ministry would require huge investment for the purchase of hardware and software. One solution that was found to be workable was for the government to enter into arrangements for leasing of computers. This would reduce the initial heavy capital investments. The State felt that lease charges could be substantially brought down by the Finance Ministry by extending the concession under the Income Tax Act, so that any investment made in IT systems would be eligible for 100 per cent depreciation in the first year itself. The leasing companies could be persuaded to provide these systems at an interest rate that would be attractive. Once this is done the departments could proceed with the leasing of computes in a big way. The funding could be arranged through agencies such as Infrastructure Leasing and Financial Services (ILFS) and Infrastructure Development Finance Corporation (IDFC) and other financial institutions.

Use of Hindi

The importance of giving access of information in Hindi was kept in mind on which count not much difficulty was envisaged since there already exist technologies such as GIST and language software by which transliteration from English into other languages can be made.

Identifying Departments with Maximum Citizen Interface

Government departments which have maximum interaction with the public had to be identified for priority attention regarding the use of IT. The following departments and activities were considered:

Public Grievances

Electricity, Water, Telephone, Ration Card, Sanitation, Public Transport, Police, etc.

Rural Services

Land Records, Below Poverty Line (BPL)/EWS families.

Police

- FIR Registration, Lost and Found
- Valuables, Persons, Dead Bodies

Social Services

- Pension
- Old Age, Widows, Ex-gratia Scheme
- Acquisition/Rehabilitation and Compensation
- Registration of Licences and Certificates
- Ration Cards, Birth Certificates, Death Certificate, Domicile Certificate, Caste/Tribe Certificate, Arms Renewal, Registration of Documents, School Registration, University Registration, Motor Vehicle Registration, Driving Licence

Public Information

- Employment Exchange Registration, Employment Opportunities, Examination Results, Hospitals/Beds Availability/Services, Railway Time Tables, Airline Time Tables, Road Transport Time Tables, Charitable Trusts, Government Notifications, Government Forms, Government Schemes

EWS Services

- Civil Supplies, Old Age Pension, Widow Pension, Handicapped Pension/Services, Ex-gratia Payment

Agriculture Sector

- Seeds Information, Pesticides, Fertilizers, Crop disease, Weather Forecast—short range /Districtwise, Market Price

Utility Payments/Billing

- Electricity, Water, Telephone

Commercial

- Taxation and Return Filing, Income Tax, Corporate Tax, Customs Duty, Central/State Excise Duty, Sales Tax, House Tax, Property Tax, Octroi, Road Tax, Company Returns

Government

- Electronic Procurement, Education University Model for E-Governance.

Connectivity

The implementation of the various schemes, however, has been slow. The Schemes of LAN and WAN connecting all Secretariat buildings and sections of the State Secretariat received sanction only in February 2003. The sanctioned schemes included setting up of computer labs for imparting computer training to the officers and employees.

The UP Portal

The setting up of the UP Portal has made it possible to access a lot of valuable information relating to the State with ease and user-friendly approach. The existence of a rich and interactive portal is one of the important dimensions of E-governance. The UP Portal has a lot of static information of a general nature and also some specific information that may be of use to specialized users. Its home page contains a news section also which gives out the headlines and important news of the day. It also has links to a major English language paper and a major Hindi newspaper. The page lists items and links which take the surfer to further pages for more detailed information as below:

Uttar Pradesh

Profile, Major Towns, Upcoming Events, Weather, Links and Resources, More…

Daily News

Current News, Editorials, More...

History

Ancient History, Middle Ages, More...

Politics

Political History, Chief Ministers of U.P., Political Parties, The Big Wigs, More…

Culture

Cultural History, Fairs and Festivals, Handicrafts, Cuisine, More…

Tourism

A-Z of Tourist Spots, Religious Tourism, Wild Life, Travel Desk, More...

Infrastructure

District, Road and Industrial Maps, Industrial Scenario and Policies, IT Initiatives, Transport, Financial Institutions, More...

Education

Schools, Universities, Technical Institutions, More...

Services

Data Services, Root Finding, IT Consultancy, More…

Directories

Rajya Sabha Members, Council of Ministers, Uttar Pradesh Police, More...

Sports

Cricket, Hockey, More...

Further details are available on clicking the main items, e.g., on the item—

Profile of Uttar Pradesh
Brief sketch of major towns
Upcoming events
Weather of major towns
Links to other U.P. related websites
What do the newspapers say
Maps
Available Infrastructure
Industrial Scenario and Policies
IT Initiatives
Power Scenario
Transport
Major Sellers and Buyers
Investment Scenario
Economy
Financial Institutions
Government Bodies
Non-biodegradable Waste Recycling
Major Industrial Centres
National Highways
Land Utilisation

Distance between Important towns and other Information

An interesting and useful feature which is extremely user friendly is the field for getting distance between two selected towns of the state.

Important towns of the State have been listed for instant information regarding the distance. But the clicking also at once furnishes a lot of links for getting information about these two towns and much more. For example, for finding the distance between Agra and Kanpur, the reply is:

Agra	Kanpur
STD-0562	STD-0512
PIN-282001, 283001	PIN-208001

Clickable Links

History of Agra	History of Kanpur
The Taj	Accessibility
More to see	Services and Utilities
Transport in Agra	Places of Interest
Shopping in Agra	Excursions
Special Events & Organised Tours	Accommodation
Increasing Pollution	
Accommodation	
Worth a Look	
How to Reach	
Get in Touch	
Eat Outs	
Excursions	
IPS Officers posted in Agra	IPS Officers posted in Kanpur
Utility Services	Utility Services
Directories	Major Sellers and Buyers
Central Cabinet	Exporters
State Cabinet	Trading Houses
Lok Sabha Members	Miscellaneous
Vidhan Sabha Members	Maps
Rajya Sabha Members	Travel Desk
Governor	Profile of UP
Judiciary	Investment Scenario

Mayors and Chief Town Officers	Handicrafts
IAS/District Officers	Cuisine
Media	UP related websites
Prominent Industrialists	Online Darshan
	Economy
	Weather
	Season's Greetings
	E-Greetings
	Travel Discounts
	Tenders

However, the aspect of dynamic information relating to government programmes, statistics or services is rather weak. Updating is done quickly for news and other items of general nature which can be accessed from many other sites as well but the information dissemination for government activities needs to be improved.

On-line Darshan

The UP Portal has a unique item of Virtual On-line 'darshan' and 'pooja' of some selected deities presiding at Ayodhya, Mathura, Vindhyachal, Varanasi and Vaishnodevi. There is a good multimedia presentation with the deity image and the ritual tools like the temple bell, flowers, *agarbattis* and *arti* lamps. On various clicks, these items get animated and create the effect of a real action on the screen.

GIS and Computer Applications—The Mirzapur Experience

In the Mirzapur town a new experiment was undertaken to administer property tax and other civic services by using the Geographical Information System (GIS) and computers and to convert it into a model, electronically administered township. The Ganga Institutional and Community Development Project (ICDP) was initiated with

Dutch support to help the municipalities of Kanpur and Mirzapur in improving the level, quality and management of urban services and infrastructure.

Legislation devolving self-government powers to municipalities was enacted by the state in 1994 requiring municipalities to assume responsibility for providing a basic level of urban services and to generate most of the revenues needed to restore urban services, which had gradually broken down. The city of Mirzapur with a population of 2,00,000 was chosen as a test case for developing a strategy to address these fundamental changes in municipal administration.

The success in the Mirzapur experiment was achieved because it was realised in the beginning that it is necessary to focus on administrative and organisational changes needed to implement works, improve financial and accounting systems, and increase revenue. This required the performance of municipal staff to be improved on a routine and not episodic basis through the introduction of appropriate work responsibilities as well as training on practical applications of municipal work.

The importance of the training of the staff and the change in attitude and approach to work was aptly summarised by Scott Gobbons that *E-Governance can be initiated through technology but it can be sustained only through E-babus* in the 29th Technical Report on the project.

The important action stages through which the project passed were:

1. Computerisation of property records, which involved location, computerisation and restoration of 23,950 property data base. This was done through a property enumeration and assessment survey during which old city maps were used to locate all properties in the city.
2. A computerised tax billing system was set-up to use the existing tax records. This made it possible to issue tax bills in the first year of the programme. Computerised billing tripled tax collection in 4 years, but since the base was 35 years old revenues were still far too low.

3. Relocation of the tax department to new offices in 2000 and the integration of the department with the computerised information system that had been operating in parallel with the old handwritten system for the previous 4 years.
4. Establishment of the Municipal Development Fund (MDF) as an independent entity and to contribute to the development of management reforms and improved project design initiated by the Municipal Support Unit.
5. Extraction of individual revenue wards from the city base map and linking with the property tax records thus establishing Municipal GIS, for the first time in the country. (The enumeration identified 44 per cent more properties than currently on the tax records).
6. A random sample of properties was checked by manual calculation to verify the formula assessment values and adjustment factors were established for the entire city.
7. Existing infrastructure records for water distribution and drainage were added to the new GIS. This was the traditional approach of using existing paper records as layers on the GIS. Initially, the street network was not the map foundation but after collecting the existing infrastructure information, the usefulness of a street network became apparent.
8. Surveys of the water and drainage systems were conducted to update conditions of recently built and mapped facilities and to establish for the first time the map location and condition of the vast bulk of the municipal infrastructure system. It then became possible to think about the various urban infrastructure as a single system with relationships between the different elements.
9. The new infrastructure data base on the GIS was first used to extract a water distribution network for modelling. A programme of water supply improvement and regularisation of connections was envisioned. These computerised records were added to the GIS to reconcile with current property tax records. This was possible for only a part of water connections.

10. The GIS was used to identify the specific infrastructure links where the least cost integrated water and drainage improvements could be made.

The final benefit areas of the experiment include several other aspects of civic services like garbage collection, city transport system and street address system for postal purposes. The success of the Mirzapur Model City approach has encouraged cities such as Vrindavan, Bangalore and Gorakhpur to implement elements of the programme. The lesson that emerges from this experiment is that a sustained result in E-governance can only come when the personnel involved have been taken initially through a process of capacity building and change of attitude with inculcation of commitment to improvement in the services rendered to the citizens.

Nine

Issues in E-Governance

Evolution of E-governance is a complex process involving a number of dimensions. Fast changing technologies have often outsmarted the efforts of governments, which are generally conventional, and, with a few exceptions, move rather slower than the markets or commercial tracks of technology. But E-governance is not driven by technology alone. All successful models of E-government or E-governance have used technology only to assist the achievement of well-conceived and sharply perceived service delivery and information dissemination goals. And, wherever E-government practices have been introduced only because it is the 'in' thing, it has faced hurdles and has reached a slowdown even before full implementation of the initial stage itself.

In India, the overview on E-governance would show that the scenario is a curious mix of achievement, intent and wishful narration of possibilities. The progress has been uneven, as there is lack of commitment and concomitant action to translate policy into reality in many of the states. There is a wide variation in computerisation rate and the actual use of IT-enabled applications within and outside the government. The disparities are also present in the various organs of the central government with different departments giving their own interpretation to the Citizen's Charter, Service Standards to be provided and the extent to which information is to be made available to the public.

There are some remarkable success stories of excellent delivery systems of information and services developed by government agencies. Out of several E-governance initiatives kicked off so far, a highly successful, user friendly, and stable IT application is the passenger reservation and information system of Indian Railways, which is also one of the oldest. There is perhaps no other case where we can find E-governance usage for such a large organisation available to the public in a reasonably user-friendly manner. Another is the portal of the Supreme Court and High Courts where information on cases and other material is available on-line. Also, there have been commendable efforts in states like Andhra Pradesh, Karnataka, Maharashtra, Gujarat, Madhya Pradesh and Himachal Pradesh underlining the very important lesson that E-government comes fast where there is imagination, creativity, commitment and attitudinal flexibility.

The slow movers, whether they are departments or the states are the cause of concern because they will distort the ICT mesh and the benefits that can flow out of the use of technology. Those states, where people have seen the benefits would usher in new services, which in turn will increase the expectations or demands of the people. Nevertheless, the big picture of E-governance is hazy because it was never ever conceived, as such. Computerisation in the government was introduced with a different motivation altogether than more effective and convenient delivery of services and information to the people.

Fundamental Questions about E-governance

There are a few basic questions about E-governance in India that have not been answered:

1. Whether common people want E-governance?
2. If so, what are their perceptions and needs?
3. Whether those who govern, administer and manage, really want E-governance?
4. What is the main objective of E-governance or E-government?

5. How to determine the priority order for ushering in the E-government systems?
6. What should be the extent of government funding of E-governance systems?
7. How prepared are we for 'change management'?
8. At what pace can the system-change take place?
9. How to bridge the already widening gap of digital divide?
10. What is the destination scenario, say ten years hence?

These are not academic questions but are the most vital ones at the present stage of E-government in India. Having started with a lot of ambition and noise making, the real achievements have been far from what was articulated and prophesied. Obviously, there is something wrong in the understanding of the best approach and methodologies. At the same time, the success stories, specially those in the initial phase of use of IT in the government, when the term 'E-governance' was not in currency, should provide insight into the whole process and factors which created the success should be assembled again to enlarge the areas of E-governance.

Whether Common People want E-governance?

On the important question whether common people want E-government or E-governance, it may be said that in a society like India that is complex and so highly stratified, it is difficult to discern common perceptions that may, by and large, represent the common view of the people or the view of the common people on such an issue. Nevertheless, it may be said that the so called common people would welcome the system if it generates convenience of procedures and saves time and harassment at the hands of the government functionaries. However, it has to be ensured that it provides them total solution and avoid face-to-face contacts with authorities as much as possible. The problem with many of the services supposed to have been initiated in India is that they provide convenience or simplification of only a few steps in the procedural jungle.

The other aspect of the people's wanting or not wanting E-governance is the question of the digital divide, meaning access to computers, computer literacy and choice about using the yet untested tool of interaction with the government and also the extra cost involved in these new services. People who are in the upper strata, globalised in outlook and practices, and are computer literate, are likely to be greatly in favour of digitised governance since their willingness to submit to the regours of procedures and confronting petty functionaries is minimal. They would like the electronic intervention in the processes of government in a big way. On the other hand, the vast humanity, specially in the rural and small town areas that does not have much to do with government is likely to remain untouched by any such facilities or the lack of them. The presence of information kiosks and on-line information systems do not impress them at large. Such a segment of population would not be insignificant and one could make an intelligent guess of this segment being about 70 per cent or more of the total numbers.

Another dimension of the issue, that never finds a mention in any government document on E-governance, is the presence of huge mass of unrecorded business transactions in the retail trade, services and taxable commodities. Real estate and related transactions are also largely done on two tracks, one of which is never made public. It is not that people do this out of any pleasure, but the total effect of this on E-commerce is highly restrictive. This segment will never submit to a regime of cent-per-cent electronically handled transactions.

People in general are quick to accept systems which they perceive to be useful to them. Some of the examples are the spread of the cable networks, mobile phones and the courier systems. Therefore, people will accept the E-governance systems and ask for more if it meets their needs as perceived by them and not by the technocrats or bureaucrats.

Whether Government Functionaries Want E-governance?

A blunt short answer to this question is that government functionaries are willing to bring change and accept it so long as their power and authority remains intact. There are also those who have vested interest in perpetuating the complex and harassing procedures as it brings them personal gains on the side. These are, unfortunately, the unstated and invisible bottom lines that will drive the advent of E-government.

Resistance by the lower functionaries or their lack of interest is not peculiar to India only. Many countries have faced this problem. One of the ways to overcome this is to allow the older or alternate service and information windows to exist side by side so that the comparative advantages become apparent. This is what has been done even in the countries that are leaders of the E-governance revolution and it is certainly the course necessary in India. However, in those countries, the E-systems are bound to be proved more people friendly and useful with the result that the older system could be phased out in a few year's time. In India, however, there is an inherent danger that people may not find the E-systems more convenient for various reasons and may feel inclined to use the older systems in spite of the availability of the new systems. That would be the end of enthusiasm about E-governance and the reversion to the old, time tested, iron-hard procedures would please the government functionary immensely. This analysis may sound pessimistic but it is only cautionary to provoke the designers of the E-government delivery systems.

Objectives of E-governance

Objectives of E-governance have never been clearly stated in India. Let us not consider the earliest stages of computerisation when the objective was better record management and cutting down on unnecessary labour and drudgery. Thereafter, during the period of networking by the National Informatics Centre, the objective was to bring national connectivity upto the district levels all over the country which was prompted by the absence of reliable telecommunication system upto the district levels. This was for the convenience of the administration, as the railways were for the convenience of the British government in the initial stage in the middle of the nineteenth century. In both these stages, *the people were nowhere in the picture.*

In the next stage, when the IT revolution had started happening in many parts of the world and it was felt necessary to derive the benefits of this new wonder tool, the National Task Force which was set up in the wake of the *'need of giving a push to the IT industry and the applications in a big way'* came out with a number of far reaching suggestions for the boost to the IT industry. It also took note of the possibilities of improving the government-people interface and suggested that Government-wide electronic information infrastructure should be created to *'simplify service delivery, reduce duplication, and improve the level and speed of service to the public'.* This was the basis of all further efforts but it did not stand out as a suggested policy statement nor as one of the main objectives of ICT applications in government functioning.

The suggestions made by the Task Force and the Working Groups constituted by it covered a vast area but instead of drawing a full picture, it made a large number of itemized and disjointed suggestions without establishing logical links with the existing processes and limitations of governance and field realities. It is this factor which has resulted in a hotchpotch growth of E-government areas in the country.

Some State Governments, like Andhra Pradesh have, later on, defined the objectives and purpose of using IT in the government processes. The latest Andhra policy document on IT mentions that electronic governance would bring in the following benefits:

- Anywhere, anytime services to citizens
- Better accountability, responsiveness and transparency
- Highly efficient government machinery and systems
- Reduced direction and arbitrariness

Even a state like Mizoram has tried to establish objectives and purpose of computerisation in the government and using IT as mentioned below but it is not as focused and operational as in the case of Andhra Pradesh which has a long and intensive experience in E-government.

Mizoram objectives are:

- Improved quality of service to citizens
- Improved efficiencies within the Government
- Better enforcement of law
- Education and information dissemination
- Enabling Government of Mizoram to provide better service and responsive administration tuned to the needs of the people
- A knowledge driven society

Which Services or Departments Should be Taken up First?

The National Task Force had itemised certain services for being taken up by the government and also indicated some other enabling actions. It appears that these were based primarily on what was being done elsewhere in the world or what was imagined to be useful in Indian context. Unfortunately, this was not preceded by any survey or study nor the needs and perceptions of the people were ascertained.

It is obvious that computerisation and use of ICT cannot be taken up all at once in all the departments. Some sort of prioritisation will have to be done but it is not wise to go in for ad-hoc decisions based on individual perceptions or the 'administrative ease'. Andhra Pradesh realized that islands of computerised systems would not do any good and would rather create problems of inter-operability. They initiated a systematic study to determine the priorities. The methodology involved:

- An exhaustive ground level survey of the governance practices within the major departments and agencies.
- Logical grouping of departments, based on comparable objectives.
- Mapping of the core processes of the departments.
- Working out the Feasibility Matrix for each group.

This methodology or any other variant should invariably be the guiding principles for laying the E-government structure. In this process of prioritisation, one has also to provide high priority for the information infrastructure. Robert Schware, Senior Informatics Specialist in the Global Information and Communications Technology Department of World Bank feels that the usual prioritisation—education and health first, information infrastructure second—is no longer valid. Just as roads are vital to bring teachers to schools or supplies to hospitals, IT is necessary to ensure the quality and accessibility of health and education. The choice cannot be health or IT, education or IT. It must be health, education and IT.

Funding of E-governance

Initial processes of computerisation and creating facilities have necessarily to be funded by the government. However, after a certain stage, it has to become a self-sustaining proposition, otherwise all the money spent in transforming or building up systems would not only go waste but may result in the collapse of service. This has also been stated in the Report of the Working Group on Convergence and E-governance for the Tenth Five Year Plan.

Ministry of Information Technology initiated a project which was aimed at using IT for masses. Earlier, in the Ninth Plan, Community Information Centres were set up in the north east and some other states for bringing ICT capabilities nearer to the people and serve the local needs. There has been no evaluation of any of these projects to see if they are actually serving the purpose and whether people are making use of these facilities for the purposes for which they were set up. It also needs to be evaluated as to what is the impact of the power situation and how the solutions devised for overcoming these problems have worked.

In the Tenth Plan, there was a proposal and also earmarking of funds for setting up some 1000 such centres all over the country. The investment proposed was of the order of abut Rs. 700 crore. There are many pitfalls like the problem of power supply to that of proper maintenance and fixing the machines in the case of any defect or malfunctioning and of the returns being able to sustain the centres on a long-term basis. If these centres cannot sustain financially, the system would start wobbling and gradually would wither away. There is a need to feel cautioned that such centres cannot be perpetually funded by Central Government and it is necessary to involve the state governments actively besides creating stakes for other agencies like the colleges, local Panchayats, youth organisations and market agencies so that they are not only sustainable but expand and grow in future on their own rather than living a life dependent on government support. If they present advantage to the people in general, all such agencies would feel interested and the centres would grow. On the other hand, if they were stereotyped, with not much of local linkages or inspiring relevance, they would not sustain, in spite of government funding.

There are examples of private participation in E-government activities as demonstrated in Andhra Pradesh, Karnataka and some others. These have to be emulated with necessary slants required by local conditions and levels of IT development. There is a need to review the total methodology of attaining E-government goals and not to treat the entire exercise as a technocratic problem that can be handled by IT professionals by themselves. According to a World Bank evaluation, of all the factors that contributed to the success of the CARD in Andhra Pradesh, effective change management clearly emerged as the most important. In fact, when asked about the manner in which the manager of the CARD project had to distribute his time and effort, he attributed 45 per cent to change management, 35 per cent to the re-engineering of processes, a mere 15-20 per cent to software, and 5 per cent to other factors (*wwwl.worldbank.org/publicsector/egov/cardcs.htm*). The AP Government decided that such projects will be led only by public administrators who have been trained to understand technology, rather than by technical specialists trained to manage. In a huge and costly demonstration of commitment to this ideal, the government has set aside funds to interview, select, and train promising public administrators for future projects. This could enlarge the methodologies beyond technological issues only.

How Prepared are we for Managing Change ?

It is not proposed to attempt an answer to this question here as this is a major issue by itself which has to be considered in depth while preparing a roadmap for marching towards electronic government. It is simple to understand that the situation is not the same all over the country and it is natural that it is so. The issue here is not of 'E-readines', which, although not studied methodically, has been at the back of the minds of the planners and executers. The question of managing change goes much beyond computing and networking.

The benefits of E-governance can come only when there is a genuine attempt to improve 'governance'. There is no visible sign of this being seriously considered anywhere, although the shortcomings in the systems have been pointed out endlessly now even in formal documents of the Planning Commission.

Our E-governance projects initiated centrally have been hardware oriented. In an analysis, NASSCOM has concluded that despite some islands of excellence, E-governance has not been able to make rapid progress due to several operational, economic, personnel, planning and implementation issues. E-governance in India has focused heavily towards investing in hardware and very little on developing software and services, which could maximize hardware investments. Hardware orientation is seen not only in the E-governance activities but there are many instances of costly equipment lying unused for long periods in the laboratories and hospitals. This is the outcome of a system where plan performance is judged by expenditure and it is considered to be an achievement if the money is spent. All this is so because we tend to equate *change* with *acquisition* of tools and do not bother much about the actual use and output of the tools. This is a problem of governance and until and unless we learn to bring change to the processes, procedures and attitudes in the government, there is very little that the 'E' in the phrase E-government would be able to do. In fact there is a danger of creating greater confusion and duplication than there was in a situation when ICT was not available for governance.

Digital Divide

Society is divided into two segments with respect to the question of being able to reap the benefits of the ICT presence and of the electronic government. Those who are on the upper side of the dividing line, often referred to as 'haves', consist of:

(a) Those who have access to computers and networks;
(b) Those who have enough skill and motivation to use computers and networks.

The 'have-nots' in this sense are those who are not in the above category. This is what defines the digital divide.

According to a survey, conducted under US government authority, in September 2001, approximately 143 million Americans were using the Internet, i.e., about 54 per cent of the population was benefiting by this new tool of technology. Regarding, the use of computers, 174 million people, or 66 per cent of the population in the United States, used computers. The younger group comprising children and teenagers were the most prolific users of computers and Internet inasmuch as about 90 per cent of children between the ages of 5 and 17 used computers. The rate of growth has been phenomenal and with each passing day more and more people are getting on to Internet and computers. A new kind of culture is fast overtaking the society in the developed countries.

The situation in India, without quoting statistics, can be described as a setting where a small segment of those who are above the divide are convinced about the utility of the use of ICT in all walks of civil life, particularly those who live in metropolitan towns and are generally well provided for. These cities are well networked, have reasonably good infrastructure for the switchover of the services from manual to electronic and where entertainment is an important part of daily existence which is because of comparatively high income levels.

The working group on IT for masses constituted by the Government of India approached the problem of E-governance only from the broadest angle and, whereas, what it said in its approach that the computerisation of front offices be taken up first rather than computerisation of the back offices is an important guideline, it has rather taken a simplistic view of the whole issue.

For one, it is not right to label the 'masses' or 'common man' as something different from the 'people' and create an impression *ab-initio* that ICT so far has been *'of the elite, for the elite and by the elite'*. In no other country have ICT applications progressed separately for segments of society. Public services are for all the people and if well-conceived high standard services are introduced, they should be such that they touch the largest number of users.

One reason why the very concept of 'masses' had to be brought in was that the ICT based services introduced in the initial stages in big cities were such that touched only the higher segments and that too did not meet everyday requirements. For example, driving licences are to be renewed only once in ten years (five in some cases) and even if one had to undergo rigors and harassment at the hands of the petty officials in the machinery, it was to be faced only once in several years. Same is the story about land registration and transfers etc. Whereas, there is absolutely no harm in computerising these services, they need not have been among the very first to be taken up. This was because of the earlier approach in the governments to computerise records and then see what services can be delivered out of them.

Computers cannot be forced on the people but they will themselves ask for them when advantages are seen and they are *affordable.* The process would gain a momentum of its own if the right kick is given initially. The availability of appropriate computing systems at affordable prices is the key consideration for government to intervene and take appropriate action rather than going in for mere acquisition of available high cost systems. Research efforts should be redoubled on placing cheap computers in the hands of the masses which can be appropriately actuated by the illiterate or low literacy population.

With several forms of divides existing in India which have remained largely unabridged, it would be futile to expect that the digital divide will be narrowed down quickly or by ad-hoc and patchy approach. The problem has several dimensions and above all the question of sustained availability of resources and capability to keep pace with obsolescence.

In some states, who have divised their own supplementary strategies and attempted creation of an effective E-government environment have succeeded better if they have gone in for assessing the perceptions and requirements of the rural people first and involved them in the process. Centrally generated programmes have been rigid and casual at the same time.

A proper strategy to bridge the digital divide should involve the following actions, in as many of simultaneous loops as may be possible. The steps should be:

- Working fast for removing the digital divide in the government itself.
- Facilitating E-delivery of services from the private sector at the grassroots levels by encouraging penetration of solution providers and the attendant culture to small towns and rural areas.
- Taking a detailed look at the facilities of maintenance and supply or computer and other IT related components and services available and work out 'human and material IT resources' budget at the district or sub-district levels with projections for coming years.
- Encouraging setting up of backroom operations of international companies in small towns and rural areas since they have shown a preference of metropolitan towns only.
- Commercial production of cheaper computers, palm tops, simputers or whatever other forms and improvements are possible should be encouraged and a culture of optimised capacity machines, specific to the requirements should be found out. In other words, embedded systems should be produced and popularised in a big way.

Extension Issues

In India, the green revolution has ridden in on the wheels of all-pervasive extension efforts, bringing to the people awareness and motivation to take to improved agricultural practices. The results are known to all that the country has been transformed into a surplus food producer in a comparatively short span of time. ICT provides a similar opportunity not only to the general public but also to business and administration. Its implications and benefits are much wider. Extension strategies are not part of IT, they require knowledge and commitment of a different kind than commitment to technology alone and that is where the approach has gone wrong in India at the central level, preventing maximisation of results in spite of all the human and technical resources being available in abundance. So long as the technical manpower that is in command of ushering in the E-governance era in India shows reluctance to submit to wider dimensions and adjusting its approach to seeing the boundaries of its turf more clearly, the progress will remain tardy and unbalanced.

Extending any technology to masses will require full involvement of the states. Centralised visualisations and uniform prescriptions would do more harm than good. It has already resulted in creation of hype before achievements in those states who have just tried to use the central template for their IT and E-government policies. On the other hand, those states which have gone by the local perceptions of the needs and priorities have showed a better scenario. However, in a totally state driven situation, there is the problem of standards and interoperability of systems that should be tackled by the Central Government or more preferably by a central independent authority.

In creating newer services, the direct role of the government technologists is dwindling and it is being replaced by market solution providers. The government has now to concentrate on the changed paradigm and conceptual aspects of delivery of services and information to its citizens. It is rather unfortunate that the procedural re-engineering aspect of governance are not being tackled. There is not much visible evidence anywhere that procedures are being made simpler or citizen friendly.

It may be interesting to refer to evaluator studies of E-governance projects conducted by some well known institutions like the IIM Ahemdabad. A common feature of all successful E-governance projects is that they have succeeded primarily because of the commitment and dedication of the 'project champions' and their teams. The teams in cases of such projects have tried to design new working procedures and created results. Prof. T.P. Rama Rao of IIM Ahmedabad observes:

> "Successful E-governance projects involved, in the design process, all stakeholders such as government officials, legislators, regulatory agencies, citizens, voluntary organizations, technology consultants and vendors, academics, researchers, funding agencies, and media."

So far in India, it has not become a routine where all or most functionaries become stakeholders as a matter of normal functioning. And, it is not realised that it is not primarily a technological exercise.

Information Literacy

The Association of College and Research Libraries (ARCL) defines Information Literacy as a set of abilities to recognise when information is needed and to have the ability to locate, evaluate and use needed information effectively. This becomes relevant in the context of the concept of 'Information Power' and 'Knowledge Power' which is fundamental to the goal of creating an Information Society and making the country a knowledge superpower. In the unfolding new paradigms, IT literacy assumes an equally important role and ability to use computers or similar devices is the essence.

In those countries, where the literacy rates are low, it may appear to be a far cry to expect high IT literacy. This is a challenge that requires lateral thinking to dissociate the skill of letters from the skill of the IT-enabled resources. In India, this will be in line with traditional knowledge acquisition of which was not necessarily based on the ability to read texts.

According to Allan Martin, computer literacy has had three phases which have come one after the other during the process of the evolution and growth of the computers during the last couple of decades. In the initial stage, the objective was 'mastery' of all the aspects of computers. The second phase was that of 'application' and finally, the present phase is a 'reflective' phase. Is it possible to expect that the first two phases are given a skip and the people on the wrong side of the divide are treated to the third phase?

In India, efforts have been made, though half-heartedly to create computers that are:

- Cheap
- Have only the necessary capacity and memory
- Non-textual interfaces using images and icons
- Voice actuation
- Small size and fully portable
- Having wireless connectivity

Simputers were being designed and developed but till the writing of this paper, they have not created any noticeable presence although in principle, in the conditions prevailing in India they would have been an appropriate tool.

Technology Related Issues

It is not possible to go into technological issues in details in this chapter. However, it may be recognised that at the present stage of ICT and with the models available in the country itself and also with the approach initially adopted by the NIC, there are no serious technological issues that cannot be addressed while we go along on any model of electronic governance. The issues, in fact, relate to choosing the proper venders and collaborators for E-government segments.

Broadly, the following concerns are to be addressed while choosing technology models and solution providers:

(a) Open systems that can be operated on multi-platforms,

(b) Interoperability and scalability,
(c) User friendliness,
(d) Capability of large data management and data mining,
(e) Converged systems for transmission of data and images,
(f) Protection of Privacy,
(g) Security, digital signatures and conditional accessibility,
(h) Socio-cultural adaptability, and
(i) Language capabilities and semantic standardisation.

None of these issues seem to pose any technological challenge and technologies have readied such stage that these can be easily handled. What is necessary is to have decisions taken in respect of certain questions of standards for languages (ASCI or Unicode?) and the manner of handling meta-data.

Challenges of technology are not in creating solutions but in creating meta-designs that are simple and flexible, yet powerful and effective. The architecture can be designed provided clear-cut and comprehensive objectives are clearly stated to meet the local, regional, national and global requirements.

The Issues Relating to Obsolescence

An important aspect that has to be taken into account in all seriousness is the fast and accelerating rate of obsolescence of hardware, software and the other interfacing methods which undergo rapid changes as the market keeps on producing newer and newer devices and ideas. This can lead to a 'gradient' that is no less undesirable than the 'divide'. It may not be always possible for government driven agencies to be in possession of the state of the art equipment and that is why this issue assumes policy dimension.

In many government offices, one can find old computers with limited capabilities using software that is no longer the latest. Apart from the psychological effects that such a situation creates in the minds of those who are still working with, say, pre 386 models, the problem of compatibility often leads to wastage of efforts and loss of data if there is a frequent switching of computers and the loaded software. It may not appear to be insurmountable problem for experts, but for an ordinary worker this can result in wastage of efforts. No solution is being offered in this paper but it is necessary that the issue is considered in its entirety and a national level decision is taken in the matter to deal with the obsolescence aspects since this is going to pose a serious problem within a few years.

What should be Avoided

With the highest quality of IT related human resources available at India's command, the country is in a position to, technologically, reach any level of E-government or E-democracy and can, theoretically, attain global standards without problems. However, the size, population, illiteracy, socio-economic conditions and conflicting priorities, together with inadequate infrastructure, impose serious limitations on the practicability of many ideas that appear attractive. Added to these are the low-productivity work-culture of the government functionaries, cumbersome procedures arising out of often irrational rules and the tendency to hide information from public. The limited availability of resources is, of course, the prime constraint. In these circumstances, it is advisable to proceed with caution and not be taken in by fanciful possibilities that technology offers or what has been successful in totally different set of situations, elsewhere.

As the novelty associated with the IT applications wanes out and greater experience is gained in implementing projects, a more professional approach to planning the future course of E-governance is required, taking into account not only the technological possibilities but a large number of questions basic to the Indian conditions. Such an approach has started getting shown in some states like Andhra, where the 'big picture' and its elements have been worked out after careful data collection and analysis. This was not the case in the approach followed by all concerned at the Central and State levels in general and the result is a hotch potch situation without any clearly defined goal.

Therefore, certain types of approach and action is to be avoided, for example,

(a) Fancy sounding schemes such as Telemedicine, Smart cards for citizens, Smart cards for vehicles, Voice actuated systems etc., should not be taken up, at least for some time, till we are fully prepared in respect of foundational structures, attitudinal re-orientation, appropriate work culture and have ground experience in simpler applications and delivery of services without glitches on a sustained basis for some time.

(b) Commitment of expenditure should not be made without the full picture. It needs to be debated at the policy levels as to how much India should spend on IT. No one has the correct picture of how much is actually being spent. In the government domain the '*3 per cent of the budget on IT*' formula may have been all right as a starter when no guidelines or estimates were available. But now, when picture is much clearer about the whole game of IT in government, such an arbitrary approach would be termed amateurish. There are some knowledgeable people, who have expressed the opinion that India should not spend too much on IT. The example of Malaysia is before us where over investment in IT infrastructure has not resulted in high growth.

(c) New services should not be contemplated without drawing up a complete panel of candidate services that can be introduced. This should be discussed openly and with user segments and only then decision taken. Successful scenarios in the world have been the result of such approach.

(d) Services should not be started where only a limited number of stages can be handled electronically. It is better to place in position preparatory conditions in the concerned agencies first, with full delivery packages being the gain of the use of IT and on-line application. It is not very wise to think that the agencies, the citizens and others concerned can take a leap from a primitive manner of functioning to the state of the art stage in one jerk, only because certain things are now technologically possible.

(e) These also imply that no hype should be created in respect services in the E-governance domain by making premature announcements and arousing public expectations before everything is ready to launch them. In the long run this becomes counterproductive.

National Council for E-governance

The co-ordination at the national level has not received the attention that it deserves. An example would serve the purpose. In the first week of November 2001, a big national conference on E-governance was organised at Goa. This was a major opportunity for taking stock of the achievements and foreseeing the pitfalls by all stakeholders. The meet, which was organised by the Department of Administrative Reforms did not have any representation from the Ministry of Information Technology. This approach is something that does not augur well for E-governance in the country.

Since the furtherance of E-governance requires fullest involvement of the states on the one hand and of all the Ministries and Departments of the Central Government on the other, a high level co-coordinating agency must be placed in command to monitor the situation and give policy directives to all concerned, convincingly and fast. The canvass is too wide to be the responsibility of within the scope of authority of a single ministry or department of the government.

The body being suggested here is not in the nature of a statutory regulatory authority, that is a more specific area of operation. The national level body should be in the nature of a Council headed by the Prime Minister or the Deputy Prime Minister and should have the Chief Ministers of the states as their members. It should be serviced by a separate and permanent secretariat.

Second Phase E-governance Policy

A time has come when it is necessary to take a fresh look at the entire E-governance scenario in the country. Drawing from experience so far and taking into account the demands of the future, a fresh

E-governance policy frame should be worked out. Several successful nations have gone on a progression in this manner in the matter of E-governance. We should also do it before it is too late and before the negative consequences of patchwork start showing up and present a more entangled public delivery system that before we ventured on the use of modern technologies in our governance and administration.

Ten

Summary and Recommendations

1. The last decade of the twentieth century has seen a very rapid development and spread of Communication and Information Technologies (ICT) along with the advent of user-friendly computing systems and networking. Governments have been quick to pick up its applications for providing better information and services to the people. Business and Industry have come to depend on the new applications in a big way.

2. Use of electronics in government and business started more than forty years ago. The advent of the Personal Computer (PC) has, in fact, brought about a revolution in the way work is transacted at public and private offices.

Governance Concepts

3. There is no agreed or settled definition of 'government' but it is understood as a process. The concept of 'governance' goes beyond that of 'government' which may not involve the citizens at all and yet do all that is necessary for the orderly existence of a society.

4. The World Bank has developed six indicators of governance, namely, Voice and Accountability, Political Stability/No violence, Government Effectiveness, Regulatory Quality, Rule of Law and Control of Corruption. It has laid great stress on the state of governance since there is a link between growth and good governance.

5. India's percentile ranking is 48 for Effectiveness, 37.7 in Regulatory Quality and 44 in Control of Corruption according to a World Bank sponsored survey.

6. Legacy structures of administration, inherited by several colonial countries, were never designed to act as machinery for growth and development with practically no concern for the convenience or the involvement of the citizens. India is a typical example where, in spite of all capabilities, government-citizen interaction has been painful and unfriendly. Bureaucracy, at all levels has a tendency to hide information from the citizen and convert this into a tool of harassment and side gains.

7. Good and helpful behaviour, transparent method of decision-making and a concern for the citizen can appreciably take out the frustrating consequences and pain of cumbersome procedures.

8. The power of the ICT has permitted the governments to adopt a 'linked-up' or 'holistic' approach by connecting various departments and organs of the government as never before. It has also provided external linkages facilitating exchange of information with other organs of the civil society and in turn disseminating information and data universally.

9. Non-governmental agencies including business, industry, educational and research institutions, have taken to ICT in a much more pervasive fashion and there the spread has been much faster than in the governments.

10. Electronic tools and networking have made it possible to involve the citizen in decision-making. In most E-government models there is considerable reduction of internal organizational friction.

11. The further evolution of use of ICT has led to what is described as E-governance, whose intimate dimensions include E-Commerce, E-Democracy, and E-Citizen.

Global Scenario of E-governance

12. There are three main models of E-government, viz., '*new economy*' model that stresses the similarities between E-government and E-business focusing on delivering high quality public services; The '*E-community*' model favoured in continental

European countries which have a strong tradition of civil society and freedom of information; and *'planned economy'* model that is used in countries which traditionally deploy interventionist public sector tools to drive and shape private sector activity and investment.

13. Out of 190 countries surveyed in a study, only 17 were found to have on-line transaction capacity. Government websites, not necessarily national governmental websites, were found only in 169 countries indicating that about 21 countries did not have even a static information dissemination system through Internet.

14. In another comprehensive study, the US, comes out at the first place, Australia takes second place, UK is placed third and Canada, the fourth. India, with all its aggressive global presence of IT professionals, ranks 45th. China is at 49, in the near company of Iran, indicating that it is yet to create conditions conducive to E-business.

15. Another survey which studied 2,288 national government websites in 196 nations indicates that full technological potential of the internet is not being utilised by governments even in the leading countries. Only 3 per cent countries had public security policy and only 8 per cent offer services that are fully executable on-line.

Australia

16. Australia decided in 1997 that all appropriate Federal Government services would be provided on-line by 2001. The first phase *Government On-line* strategy, released in April 2000, mainly involved the migration of existing information services to the on-line environment. Federal agencies responded to the challenge of placing all appropriate services on-line.

17. The second phase objective was 'Better Services, Better Government' which was adopted in November 2002. In this phase citizens are at the core of the process and the objectives include delivering services that are responsive to clients and enhance closer citizen engagement.

18. Income Tax return filing on-line is becoming popular in Australia. By early November 2002, more than 5,40,000 people had

lodged their return on-line. The tax office is processing nearly 90 per cent returns within 10 days and almost 100 per cent within 14 days.

United States of America

19. The approach of the US is based on the principles of *Easy access, Re-engineered Systems, Automated Systems, One-Stop Service; Service by Customer, not Provider; Privacy protection and Access to the physically challenged.*

20. A Task Force was set-up in July 2001 which considered over 160 E-government proposals and narrowed them down to 30. The President's Management Council selected 23 of the 30 cross-agency E-governance initiatives for funding, and added a payroll processing initiative making it "24 initiatives" for E-government. Multi agency project teams prepared the implementation road map.

21. Some new legislative measures and time bound action mandates have been introduced in the recent years to provide the necessary environment and push, e.g., Government Paperwork Elimination Act of 1998 (GPEA), Electronic Signatures in Global and National Commerce Act of 1999 (E-SIGN). Health Information Protection and Accountability Act (HIPAA) and EBT Interoperability Act.

22. The official portal of the US Government offers Gateway for Citizens, Gateway for Business and Gateway for government employees.

Japan

23. Japan has aimed at creating an Advanced Information Communication Network Society, with the ability of the people to effectively utilize information. It was envisaged that by March 2004, information and processes in the computers and networks would equal that on the paper.

24. Computerisation in government in Japan started many years ago and using computers had become quite pervasive by the mid-nineteen nineties. In December 1997, the Cabinet decided on a Revised Basic Plan for the Computerisation of Government

Administration to initiate 'E-government'. In November 2000, the Basic Law for Formation of an Advanced Information-Communication Network Society was enacted.

25. The 'IT Headquarter' was installed within the Cabinet in January 2001 in accordance with the Basic IT Law and was headed by the Prime Minister himself. The IT Headquarters consisted of all Cabinet Ministers and several well-informed independent persons.

26. A comprehensive review of procedures, speeding up of the implementation of plans and projects than what was originally planned, and widespread use of electronic systems for quicker completion of administrative processing were the important actions that were taken to give full meaning to the use of ICT in the government systems and for facilitating the interaction between the citizen and the government.

27. The services already available to the citizens are in the field of electronic payment of taxes and fees, matters related to motor vehicles and driving licences. Electronic processing of applications, reports and other procedures, availability of administrative information. 24 hours a day through homepages on the Internet.

Scenario and Initiatives in India

28. Computers came to India in 1959 but were slow to catch on. There was a feeling amongst employees of the establishments introducing computers in the initial stages that it would replace workers and result in loss of jobs.

29. In 1975, the Government of India decided to introduce the use of computers in government and computer-based decision support system in the ministries and departments to facilitate planning and programme implementation.

30. During 1985-90, NIC reached out to 550 district headquarters in the country and established a nationwide ICT Network called NICNET in 1989. The Committee on Study Group on Information Gap, constituted by the Planning Commission recommended creation of databases on Plan Information, Monitoring and Evaluation in districts. Based on the NICNET, the District Government Informatics Programme (DISNIC) was taken up in 540 districts.

31. In May 1998, a National Task Force was set-up which had mandate to formulate the draft of a National Informatics Policy. A number of important recommendations were made in the three reports. It suggested earmarking at least 2 per cent of the budget of every ministry or department.

32. On the recommendations of this Task Force, government initiated several regulatory and promotion measures to remove impediments and enable the growth of IT industry in the country and to enable large-scale applications of IT in various areas related to day-to-day lives of the people. Simultaneously, the government was conscious of the possibility that these could create a new division in society, referred to as *digital divide.* Therefore, government constituted a Working Group on Information Technology for Masses on May 10, 2000 which presented a number of recommendations.

33. During the Ninth Five Year Plan period, there was stress on the total IT sector and there was no mention of E-governance. Mid-way through the Plan period came the 3 per cent mandate and the responsibility of IT industry as well as using IT in government shifted to the new Ministry of Information Technology.

34. The Tenth Five Year Plan defined the scope of E-governance and mentioned that it involves transformation from being a passive information and service provider to active citizen involvement. It was suggested in the report that the Master Plan of E-governance should develop a clearly focused vision of the objective of introducing E-governance. It included provision for development of local language tools and content, evolving IT architecture, technical support to State governments, Public Key Infrastructure, and IT for masses besides other necessary infrastructure and research needs.

Andhra Pradesh

35. Andhra Pradesh was the first State in the country to take up E-government in a systematic manner under a clear-cut vision where efforts were initiated, monitored and facilitated by the Chief Minister of the State himself. It was in 1998, when its first E-governance project, called CARDS, was initiated as computerised property title

registration and stamp duty payment service. The six main projects that have laid the foundation of E-government in Andhra Pradesh are: APSWAN, CARD, TWIN, MPHS, APDMS, SKIMS and FAST.

36. In July 2000 the Government of Andhra Pradesh initiated its Information Technology Policy 2000 arising out of its Vision 2020 document. The vision of the State for the IT sector was that Andhra Pradesh will leverage Information Technology to attain a position of leadership and excellence in the information age and to transform itself into a knowledge society.

37. With the growing realisation all over the world that good governance is necessary not only for the orderly functioning of the society but also for carrying out development and welfare measures effectively, it was broadly found necessary and possible to improve *Government-Citizen interface, Government-Business interface and Infra-Governmental processes* with the use of IT.

38. The ICT policy initiated in 2002 aimed at creating an environment for realisaton of the Vision 2020 and adoption of Information Technology in all aspects of development including E-governance.

39. A quick decision was taken on the vexed question of 'free right of way' for telecommunication purposes along highways. The process of cable laying was accelerated and the work was completed in record time.

40. Realising that computerisation and use of ICT in isolated islands would create more complications than good and that the government departments cannot follow 'stand alone' approach, the state used the enterprise approach which made state-wide perspective as the basis for designs rather than technological perspective thus attempting to synchronise multiple applications that run on a number of infrastructure components.

41. The question of the order or priority of departments for ICT applications was answered through an exhaustive ground level survey of the governance practices within the major departments and agencies. Logical grouping of departments, based on comparable objectives was done and feasibility matrix for each group was worked out. The priorities as well as the phasing of introduction of the

applications was, thus, determined through a highly scientific and professional process.

42. Public-Private Participation for E-government initiatives funding was conceived under the policy framework initiated in August 2001.

43. Standard of service was given due importance and it was declared as a component of the service delivery system.

Gujarat

44. Gujarat started a little late in the efforts to bring the benefits of ICT in governance. But it expressed a resolve to catch up fast.

45. The objective was creating transparent government so as to fulfil the citizens charter; to use IT to improve overall organisational efficiency and pass the benefits to the citizens of the state.

46. The roadmap of E-governance envisaged identification of key areas on priority basis for computerisation in each department and take up those systems first which improve the delivery systems for the citizens. Delivery time for the citizens was to be cut down demonstrably in a time-bound fashion. Creating greater convenience for the citizens through efficient and intelligent interface in the form of computer-supported counters, kiosks etc. was conceived. One per cent of the State Government budget was committed to IT related activities which was expected to rise to three per cent in the year 2005.

47. The government planned and implemented Sachivalaya Integrated Communication Network and Gujarat State Wide Area Network (GSWAN) interconnecting all administration nodes at the capital city of Gandhinagar, Districts and Talukas through end-to-end IP based network designed with all services converging on to the same system with compatibility to other existing networks in Government. The Integration of Secretariat Campus Area Network (SCAN) with GSWAN induced mutual synergy in two networks.

48. The City Civic Centre, Ahmedabad has a string of computers on the network and allows citizens to avail facilities like paying property tax, getting a death/birth certificates, file a water tap, drainage

connection request, apply for building plan approval, lodge a complaint/grievance, make miscellaneous payments etc.

49. Mahiti Shakti portals for Citizen to Government (C-G) and Government to Citizen (G-C) transactions was developed as a 'pro of concept' portal by the Concept Centre for Electronic Governance (CCEG) of the Indian Institute of Management, Ahmedabad (IIM-A) and was launched on 4th October, 2001 across 14 Mahiti Shakti Kendras (MSKs).

50. Pilot for Chief Minister's Call Centre or 'Tele Fariad' for public grievances was started in Banaskantha District in December 2001. Experience was successful and another Call Centre was commissioned for Rajkot District in April 2002.

51. The state portal is very rich and interactive and provides useful information to citizens on a variety of subjects including employment and training.

Karnataka

52. Karnataka established an Electronic City wayback in 1985, which provided entrepreneurs with land, water, incubation centre and excellent communication facilities. A Software Technology Park (STPI) was set-up in 1991, which began by servicing 13 companies which had grown to around 900 in 2003. STPI established earth stations in Mysore and Manipal. IT companies continue to chose Bangalore for location of their offices and operations because of the ready availability of world class IT infrastructure and ample supply of specialised technical manpower.

53. The State is now concentrating on developing three more places as IT growth centres, namely Mysore, Manipal and Hubli.

54. The Karnataka Government Computer Centre, which was established in 1971, was also one of the earliest in the country. The Secretariat LAN had 1500 nodes setup in the Vidhana Soudha, MS Building and New MS Building. The buildings were connected by optic fiber cable. Information requirements of the Chief Minister's office were catered by project Mukhya Vahini.

55. The departments like Agriculture, Finance, Commercial Taxation, Education, Forest, Insurance, Police, Municipal Administration etc., have their own websites and portals. Bangalore Development Authority provides services for computerised allotment of site and layout plans using GIS package through Internet.

56. Millennium IT policy was announced in order to 'refocus' and "define it in a way that is most suited for the present". One of the objectives of the policy is to "use E-governance as a tool and deliver a government that is more pro-active and responsive to its citizens". It also aims at promoting the usage of Kannada in Information Technology.

Mizoram

57. Mizoram was only a district of the undivided Assam till 1972. It has transited from a state of armed insurgency to a land of absolute peace. It has the second highest literacy rate in the country and a forward looking people. With improved communication and connectivity it shows promise in several sectors including IT and E-governance.

58. First initiatives were taken in 1991 with the establishment of an Electronics Cell in the Directorate of Industries and the Zoram Electronics Development Corporation Limited (ZENICS). However, the actual progress was confined to conducting training courses and nothing much happened in the field of E-government.

59. NIC is providing computer and communication based support to the State Government through its Satellite based computer communication network, NICNET. Due to limitation in the NIC infrastructure, they cannot provide Internet connection to all the Government offices at present.

60. The Government of Mizoram is planning to IT enable all the Secretariat offices for increasing quality services, reduce costs and improve overall efficiency and effectiveness in the Government. It has made proposals for various IT applications in the government offices and for delivery of services.

Uttar Pradesh

61. The IT policy of 1999 of the State aims at using IT as a vehicle for economic development and for creating a high-tech society with a high quality of life in Uttar Pradesh. There has been no use of the term 'E-governance' or 'E-government', yet the vision was to make U.P. a 'Smart State' in 10 years in so as far as IT application in Government was concerned.

62. The plan was developing NOIDA/Greater NOIDA, Ghaziabad and Lucknow as Smart Cities by the year 2000, Gorakhpur, Kanpur, Aligarh, Bareilly and Agra by the year 2002. Allahabad, Moradabad and Varanasi were to be developed into smart cities by the year 2003, rest of the Divisional headquarters by 2005 and the remaining State by the year 2008. These tall objectives, however, do not seem to have materialised.

63. The state has created the legislative provisions for optical fibre cable laying and maintenance and for private universities teaching Information Technology.

64. For meeting the requirements of large number of computers, instead of buying them, it was decided to go in for lease of these machines from private entrepreneurs who would be assisted through incentives to enter into computer leasing activity.

65. Government departments which have maximum interaction with the public were to be identified for priority attention regarding the use of IT.

66. The importance of giving access of information in Hindi was kept in mind on which count not much difficulty was envisaged since there already exist technologies such as GIST and language software by which transliteration from English into other languages can be made.

67. The UP Portal has a lot of static information of a general nature and also some specific information that may be of use to specialised users. Its home page also gives out the headlines and important news of the day. It provides links to a major English and a major Hindi newspaper.

Issues and Recommendations

68. In India, the overview of E-governance would show that the scenario is a curious mix of achievement, intent and wishful narration of possibilities. The progress has been uneven, there is a wide variation in computerisation rate and the actual use of IT-enabled applications.

69. There are some remarkable success stories of excellent delivery systems of information and services developed by government agencies in the states and the centre but there are also slow movers.

70. Computerisation in the government was introduced with a motivation different than more effecient and convenient delivery of services and information to the people.

71. Some basic questions about E-governance have never been addressed, e.g., whether common people want it and what are their perceptions and needs. Whether the government functionaries really want E-governance which will curtail their power and authority? Also, how prepared are we for managing 'change'? Coupled with these are the consequences of 'digital divide'.

72. An issue that is hardly taken into consideration is the presence of huge mass of unrecorded business transactions in the retail trade, services and taxable commodities. This segment will never submit to a regime of cent-per-cent electronically handled transactions unless several paradigms undergo change.

73. Resistance by the lower functionaries or their lack of interest is not peculiar to India only. Many countries have faced this problem. One of the ways to overcome this is to allow the older or alternate service and information windows to exist side by side so that the comparative advantages become apparent.

74. The National Task Force had itemized certain services for being taken up by the government and also indicated some other enabling actions. These were based primarily on what was being done elsewhere in the world or what was imagined to be useful in Indian context, but such a far reaching exercise was not preceded by any survey or study nor the needs and perceptions of the people and the ground realities

75. Issues relating to the funding of E-government infrastructure and further extension of services are very important for the sustainability

of the activities. Appropriate models must be developed and tried out for public-private partnership as is being done in some states.

76. The benefits of E-governance can come only when there is a genuine attempt to improve 'governance'. There is no visible sign of this being seriously considered anywhere, although the shortcomings in the systems have been pointed out endlessly.

77. E-governance projects initiated centrally have generally been hardware oriented and very little investment has gone in developing software and services, which could maximize hardware investments. Until and unless, we learn to bring change to the processes, procedures and attitudes in the government, there is very little that the 'E' in the phrase E-government would be able to do.

78. Computers cannot be forced on the people but they will themselves ask for them when advantages are seen and they are *affordable.* The availability of appropriate computing systems at affordable prices is the key consideration for government to intervene and take appropriate action rather than going in for mere acquisition of available high cost systems.

79. Suggestions for narrowing the digital divide have been made see on page 127.

80. Extending any technology to masses will require full involvement of the states. Some of those states which have gone by the local perceptions of the needs and priorities have showed a better scenario than those who have gone by centralised visualisation and prescriptions. Extension strategies are not part of IT; they require knowledge and commitment of a different kind than commitment to technology alone.

81. In creating newer services, the direct role of the government technologists is dwindling and it is being replaced by market solution providers. The government has now to concentrate on the changed paradigm and conceptual aspects of delivery of services and information to its citizens rather than treating everything as technological issue.

82. Successful E-governance projects involve, in the design process, all stakeholders such as government officials, legislators, regulatory agencies, citizens, voluntary organizations, technology consultants and vendors, academics, researchers, funding agencies, and media (Prof. T.P. Rama Rao of IIM, Ahmedabad).

83. IT Literacy becomes relevant in the context of 'Information Power' and 'Knowledge Power' which is fundamental to the goal of creating an Information Society and making the country a knowledge superpower. When literacy rate is low, it may appear to be a far cry to expect high IT literacy. This is a challenge that requires lateral thinking to dissociate the skill of letters from the skill of the IT enabled resources. In India, this will be in line with traditional knowledge, acquisition of which was not necessarily based on the ability to read texts.

84. In the present State of IT development in the country issues of technology are not about creating solutions but about creating meta-designs that are simple and flexible, yet powerful and effective. The challenge is also to develop low cost hardware for specific applications.

85. As the novelty associated with the IT applications wanes out and greater experience is gained in implementing projects, a more professional approach to planning the future course of E-governance is required, taking into account not only the technological possibilities but a large number of ground issues basic to the Indian conditions. One should not be taken in by fancy sounding schemes and they should not be taken up till we are fully prepared in respect of foundational structures, attitudinal re-orientation, appropriate work culture and have ground experience in simpler applications and delivery of services without glitches on a sustained basis for some time.

86. New services should not be contemplated without a professional analysis of the core functions of a government department or agency. A panel of 'candidate services' should be discussed openly and with user segments and only then they should be slated for introduction.

87. A high level co-coordinating agency, say the National Council for E-Governance must be placed in command to monitor the progress and give policy directives to all concerned, convincingly and fast. The governance universe is too complex to be handled by any single ministry or department of the government.

88. Drawing from experience so far and taking into account the demands of the future, a fresh E-governance policy frame should be worked out as done in many countries. We should also do it before it is too late and before the negative consequences of 'patchwork' start showing up and confront us with a more entangled public delivery system.

Appendix

EXCERPTS FROM THE INFORMATION TECHNOLOGY POLICY OF SOME STATES

Information Technology Policy of Assam, 2000 (ITPA, 2000)

(Notified vide No. MI. 102/99/11 dated the 17th June, 2000)

Introduction

Information Technology (IT) occupies a key position in our modern age and is one of the fastest growing sectors in the world economy. Application of IT have become pervasive, covering all spheres of life. Government of Assam has recognised this fact and has formulated the policy below keeping in mind all facets of IT.

Objectives of the Policy

The basic objectives of the Information Technology Policy of Assam shall be:

1. To accord primacy to the growth of Information Technology industry in the state;
2. To accelerate the use of Information Technology at the government level with a view to provide better services to the citizens of the state;
3. To improve productivity and efficiency of the Government services to the citizens of the state;
4. To serve as an important tool to enhance employability as

well as to absorb a major portion of the educated unemployed in the state;

5. To enable the state reach an eminent position in the Information Technology sector;
6. To encourage and accelerate the growth of both the domestic and the export oriented IT units in the state and make the state an attractive destination for IT investment within India and abroad;
7. To encourage and accelerate the use of Information Technology in schools, colleges and educational institutions in the state to enable the youth to acquire necessary skills and knowledge in this sector making them highly employable;
8. To set-up specialised training institutes in private sector and the joint sector in order to prepare skilled manpower within the existing system;
9. To organise Manpower Development Training Programme (MDTP) in the field of Computer Applications for the successful implementation of the Information Technology Policy of Assam;
10. To develop appropriate networks between various departments and different spatially spread out administrative hierarchies through well designed database management system; and
11. To encourage the spread of IT in the private sector.

Information Technology Policy for the Government Administration

The Industry and Commerce Department would function as nodal department for implementation of the IT policy, which would co-ordinate with all the other departments of the Government of Assam in order to ensure that the detailed objectives and goals of the IT Policy are achieved.

The Government shall endeavour to have connectivity among all its offices within 2004 so that communication can flow through E-mail/video conferencing etc. to enhance productivity. The

Government shall endeavour to provide video conferencing and E-mail facilities in all district headquarters to enable communication with the State Secretariat.

The Government shall endeavour to improve the process of governance so that citizens could file their documents required by the Government electronically. Web applications would be developed in the local language of the state.

The Government shall endeavour to put in place training programme to enable all government employees to use Information Technology to enhance productivity.

The Government shall make a special budget allocation of at least 2-3 per cent of the plan fund allocated to the Government departments every year to complete its computerisation programmes in each Department. An IT sub-plan would be formulated department-wise and closely monitored.

The Government shall improve infrastructure such as laying of communication cables for interconnecting the departments, setting up of data transfer exchanges, routers, gateways etc. and ensure reliable power supply, transport system etc. to improve the quality of works.

The Government shall encourage the use of Information Technology in all educational institutions by way of giving special grants every year to enable them to put up the necessary infrastructure. Connectivity between the various educational institutions would also be established by 2004.

The Government shall with the help of the industry start training programmes for teachers to help them use Information Technology in the teaching process.

The Government shall endeavour to teach the school level children the use of computers and to impart training through computers. All college students in the state of Assam would be encouraged to undertake three months course in the use of Information Technology and in working on computer by 2004.

The Government shall endeavour to increase the number of college students specialising in Information Technology to meet the needs of the Information Technology industry to cater to both the export and domestic market. The syllabi for specialisation in computer education would be standardised and recognised to make in more relevant. The education department would monitor the placements on offer and make suitable changes in the design of courses according to the needs of the jobs.

The Government shall strengthen the Assam Electronic Development Corporation Ltd. (AEDC Ltd.). AEDC will play the role of facilitator and assist various Government departments in selection of appropriate hardware, software and training programmes in accordance with their needs.

For specialised training in emerging areas of Computer and Communication Technology the Government shall consider sponsoring employees of various government departments, undertakings, autonomous organisations and other non-governmental organisations to institutions situated within or outside the State. All efforts would be made to set-up an autonomous HIT at Guwahati with assistance from Private sector and Union Government.

Subsidy on Quality Certification

Fifty per cent of the cost for getting ISO: 9000 Software Engineering Institute (SEI) certification and Quality Assurance Institute (QAI) certification shall be subsidised subject to a ceiling of Rs. 2 lakhs.

For mega projects the Government would consider special incentives on a case by case basis in addition to the benefits already provided. A Mega project may be define as one having investment of Rs. 100 crores and more.

Special Incentives for IT Enabled Industries

In addition to the benefits provided to IT Industries the following benefits shall be provided for IT enables services:

1. Power subsidy shall be available for a period of 5 years from the date of going into commercial production. The amount of subsidy shall be 60 per cent subject to a ceiling of Rs. 10 lakh per year.

2. The subsidy on captive generating set including non-conventional energy generation set shall be 60 per cent of the cost of the generating set subject to a ceiling of Rs. 15 lakh per industrial unit.
3. State Capital Investment subsidy of 40 per cent on the capital investment on land, building, plant and machinery etc., subject to a ceiling of Rs. 15 lakh shall be provided to an IT unit under the policy.
4. 60 per cent subsidy on shed rent payable to STPI shall be available for a period of three years from the date of going into commercial operation subject to a ceiling of Rs. 5 lakh per annum.
5. 40 per cent subsidy on Hot line/Leased line connectivity paid to STPI or VSNL, subject to a ceiling of Rs. 10 lakh per annum shall be vailable to the unit for a period of three years from the date of commercial production.

The eligibility criteria specifically for the IT enabled sector are as follows:

(a) The unit should provide employment for minimum 100 local persons.
(b) Employment should be provided for a minimum period of three years.
(c) A minimum wage of at least Rs. 4500 per month per employee shall be provided by the unit.

The Government would take all necessary steps to exempt the IT Industry from the relevant provisions of the following regulations:

(a) Factories Act, 1948
(b) Employment Exchange (Compulsory Notification of Vacancies) Act, 1959
(c) Payment of Wages Act, 1936
(d) Minimum Wages Act, 1948
(e) Contract Labour (Regulation & Abolition) Act, 1970

(f) Workmen Compensation Act, 1923
(g) Shops & Establishment Act, 1971
(b) Employees State Insurance Act, 1948
(i) Zonal Regulation under the Gauhati Metropolitan Authority Act, 1985 (Notification for zoning *vide* TCP.79/83/56 dated 25-9-1986 publish in Gazette on 24-12-1986)

Bihar Information Technology (IT) Scenario

Information Technology Policy of Bihar was not available. However, some statements on the website indicate the approach towards IT and E-governance.

State government is keen to promote IT culture throughout State in order to benefit the masses through this technology. Some computerisation activities have been carried out by the State Government with the technical support from National Informatics Centre, Bihar State Unit in various departments. National Informatics Centre, Bihar State Unit was requested to submit a Project of worth Rs. 10 crore for the improvement of overall IT infrastructure and implementation of E-governance for the State. The Project Funding was sanctioned by Planning Commission, Government of India. In response to above project, National Informatics Centre submitted a Project Proposal to the Government. The Steering Committee under the Chairmanship of Development Commissioner after several sittings passed the Project Proposal to the Cabinet for further necessary action. Subsequently, the Cabinet also approved the proposal.

Government of Haryana Information Technology Policy 2000

The State Government recognises the role of IT as an effective tool in catalysing economic activity, in efficient governance and in developing human resource. This policy seeks a deep impact initiative by the State Government in encouraging replacement of traditional delivery system of public services by IT driven system of governance that works better, costs less and is capable of serving the citizens' needs with ease. A high degree of public satisfaction through transparent and efficient functioning of public domain activities would be at the focus of IT initiative. Application of sunrise technologies in transition to a knowledge based society, providing equal opportunity to all in reaping the benefits of development, harnessing vast potential of human endeavour and enriching quality of life shall provide the long-term underpinning of socio-economic transformation of the State. This policy further seeks to facilitate private domain initiative in E-transition of Haryana by providing critical infrastructure, systems framework and enabling environment.

IT Vision—*To transform Haryana into an IT driven economy.*

Objectives

The IT Vision is sought to be realised by achieving the following objectives:

1. Upgrading the standard and quality of administration, particularly in social and public services sector through a process of modernisation and rationalisation of the administrative set up,
2. Providing public centred, efficient and cost-effective Government,
3. Extensive percolation of IT literacy and education in the State,
4. Promoting investments in IT industry,
5. Encouraging private sector initiative in IT related infrastructure and services,
6. Increasing the share of IT in State Gross Domestic Product,
7. Generating IT related employment opportunities, and
8. Enhancing earning capacity of the residents thereby ensuring a better quality of life.

Re-engineering of Administrative Processes

The State shall undertake intensive re-engineering and administrative reforms, redefining its role, and recasting the structure and functioning of its administrative departments to facilitate adaptation to IT. This exercise shall be carried by removal of redundancies, resource optimisation and rationalisation of rules and procedures to bring about transparency in working and enhancing efficiency and productivity.

IT application in transaction automation and creation of information databanks will be mandatory for all departments. Boards and Corporation to achieve accountability and efficiency in administration. This process will be completed by the year 2003.

As a part of administrative re-engineering, integration of projects across various departments to provide a single point of contact to citizens for electronic delivery of services would be put in place.

IT Initiative Fund for E-Governance

An IT initiative fund for E-governance shall be established with contributions from profit making State PSUs, co-operative institutions and other public sector organisations. The initiative fund shall be utilised for developing replicable and reusable models of E-governance, IT innovations in administration reengineering, IT supported resource optimization, decision support systems, MIS, intranets and other applicable enabling technologies.

The fund shall have an initial Corpus of Rs. 10 crores and shall be administered by a Governing Body headed by the Principal Secretary to the Chief Minister. An Executive Committee of the Governing Body headed by Secretary shall be constituted for appropriations from this fund.

State-wide Area Network

The State shall establish backbone network Haryana State Wide Area Network (HARNET) for voice, data and video transmission and dissemination. The network shall be utilised for inter department connectivity, multi-user and multi-service facilities, video conferencing, file transfer facility, e-mail, on-line application processing, query and response. HARNET shall enable better communication, information sharing, allowing people to work together more effectively resulting in cohesive administration. Phased implementation of HARNET will cover strengthening the existing intranets at State Secretariat. Haryana Bhawan and 19 district headquarters with existing NIC/DOT infrastructure. The second phase shall extend HARNET to all government separtments, state secretariat, districts, sub-divisions, tehsils, sub-tehsils and block headquarters. Hartron shall implement this extended HARNET in association with private sector. Where DOT is not in a position to provide suitable links, such connectivity shall be achieved through private initiative.

The State Government Departments shall establish departmental intranets and local area networks which will lay the foundation of Centralised Data Repository of public domain information for "Anytime-Anywhere" usage.

SMART Cards

SMART Card based citizens ID with multi-functions that enable citizens to interact with services, make payments, act as a Voter ID, obtain ration card, passport, driving licence and vehicle registration etc. shall be introduced in association with the private sector by the year 2003.

Use of Hindi

The State Government shall promote use of Hindi in Information Technology to increase the outreach to the common man. For this purpose specific initiative will be taken for use of Devnagri in computers and developing web applications.

Government Tendering/Procurement Process

Electronic procurement and settlement system with supporting databases and transparent decision making shall replace the existing system by the year 2002.

MIS for Different Levels

An efficient and effective department specific IT based Decision Support System/Management Information System shall be evolved concurrently with the process of reengineering in the state government. Abstract on all developmental parameters, revenue collections, crime rate, key agricultural inputs, condition of irrigation facilities, status of power generation and distribution, social infrastructure etc. will be integrated in this system. Wherever, citizen interface is involved, web enabled applications will be developed. On-line Analytical Processing (OLAP) would be developed for planning and decision-making. This initiative shall be supported by the Secretariat for Information Technology. The process shall be completed by the year 2003.

Standardisation of IT Infrastructure, Data and Applications

It shall be mandatory for all departments, Boards and Corporations to procure hardware, software, networking equipment etc. according to specifications and standardisation laid down by Hartron which shall be the sole agency of the State Government to procure software and equipment. General use application software like payroll, personnel information system, inventory management system, budget expenditure control, grievance handling and office automation systems, etc., shall in future be developed by Government Departments, Boards and Corporations on the technical advice of Hartron. Standardisation of data shall also be carried out by organisations to the feasible extent.

These steps shall enable integration of resources into the State Intranet, creation of 'Central Data Warehouses' and predictable architecture ensuring the manageability, portability and inter-operability of systems. These efforts shall culminate into public domain information availability on centralised servers reducing future costs of IT applications.

Use of GIS Technology

GIS shall be extensively used in integrating, analysing and visualising different types of data for spatial planning, environmental protection, utility management, traffic regulation etc. Digitised maps of Haryana already available with NIC-HSU will be utilised for providing GIS based services. Augmentation of digitised base maps shall be made as and when required.

Development of Portal Website

A Portal website of the state would be set-up by Hartron by interconnecting website of every department and organisation who in turn shall develop their own websites. The portal site developed by Hartron shall be updated dynamically. All government tenders, employment news, public domain information and notices issued by government for general public shall be published on this website.

IT Literacy in Government

The government shall implement an IT Literacy Plan (ITLP) for its employees to achieve 100 per cent IT literacy in the government by 2002. IT literacy will have a minimum level of defined proficiency which will include word processing, E-mail, data entry and access etc. Suitable incentive/disincentives shall be designed to achieve desired level of proficiency.

Each department shall create an IT Cell to be headed by Chief Information Technology Officer (CITO) who shall co-ordinate and supervise implementation of E-governance. The CITO will be a qualified computer professional. Where suitable officer is available within the department, his level of skills will be enhanced through requisite training. The departments shall undertake review of existing manpower and replace adequate number of posts with IT personnel without any additions to overall establishment budget. Senior and Middle level functionaries in the departments shall be trained in relevant IT applications and management techniques apart from achieving minimum defined proficiency level. This initiative will be supported by Hartron and NIC. All manual/electronic typewriters shall be phased out, use of e-mail, internet and computers in general shall be maximised.

E-Citizen Interface

Digitisation of Public Domain Information

All public domain information like Official Gazette notifications, Acts, rules, regulations, circulars, policies and programme documents would be digitised and made available for electronic access on Web. This process shall be completed by the year 2002.

Public Information and Facilitation Counters (PIFCs) in Government offices shall be set-up so that public domain information is available without any harassment. These PIFCs shall also function as e-mail access into **grievance suggestion databases.**

Delivery of Public Domain IT Services

The State Government proposes to establish electronic delivery of services in the public domain in its Departments, Boards and Corporations using state-of-the-art technology. Such delivery of services shall be permitted on transaction fee basis to be charged from the users. Flexibility to individual departments to fix transaction fee shall be permitted. Quality assurance for such delivery shall follow well laid out norms.

IT and Private Domain

Electronic Commerce

The development of electronic market places is transforming the structure of global economy. B2B and B2C applications like E-Banking require a number of legal issues to be addressed. The State Government will give due emphasis on E-commerce and will endeavour to develop **International Electronic Commerce Hub** in Gurgaon. This hub will be set-up in joint venture with VSNL/private sector. The State Government will remove hurdles to EC growth and development and will expedite it through joint venture pilot projects in association with the private sector. Legal framework required for speedy implementation shall be expedited.

Promotion of IT-enabled Services or Remote Services

The State Government shall promote establishment of units for providing IT-enabled Services or Remote Services as these have vast employment generation potential. Technical know-how, marketing support and financial assistance will be provided by State Government Organisations for setting up such units.

Promotion of IT Industry

The State Government recognised the need to give fillip to investments by the private sector in IT Industry. The role of the State Government shall be to facilitate such investment by creating investor friendly environment, escort services, speedy clearances and reliable infrastructure. The IT industry has already been recognised as the major thrust area under the Industrial Policy, 1999. A special package of incentives, which provide opportunity for competitive growth under this IT Policy has been specifically worked out for the IT industry.

Service Delivery Points (SDPs)

The SDPs shall be encouraged in the private sector for citizens to access services. This will include Information Kiosks, Public Tele Info Centres (PTICs), Interactive Voice Response Systems (IVRS) for interaction with databases.

Internet Community Centres

The State Government will promote setting up of Internet Community Centres by private sector to provide Internet facilities throughout the State and up to last mile linkage.

Hi-tech Habitat/ITT Complexes/Private Software Technology Parks (STP)

The State Government will set-up Hi-tech Habitat/ITT Complexes at Gurgaon, Panchkula and other candidate sites in the State. In addition, the State Government will promote setting up of private STPs by liberalising the government procedures and policies. Special encouragement shall be given to setting up of IT incubators.

Gujarat

Information Technology Policy

Mission

To help improve processes in the government by using computing devices, communication systems associated electronics and software to provide better delivery systems to the citizens.

It is very clearly understood that IT is not an end in itself but means to provide better quality of life to the citizens of the State. It does not aim at merely automating existing process but the target is to use IT to improve overall organisational efficiency and pass the benefits to the citizens of the State.

Objectives

- Over all IT growth in the state of Gujarat;
- To create enormous new employment opportunities in the State;
- To train and develop skilled manpower in IT;
- To facilitate information outlets at the doorstep of the common man to enable people at large to access information related to-education, i.e., technical and non technical course offered by various institutions, admission procedures, admission list, results, etc., health services—like various medical expertise available at different hospitals, on line medical services, etc., transport service information-like bus arrival and departure timings, reservation facilities, etc.,

Information Kiosks will also provide the on-line delivery of various application forms to the users irrespective of their location in the State.

- To make Government-Citizen interface more effective, efficient and transparent.

Information Technology in Government

The usage of IT strategies in government would be a key to improving processes which will ensure better delivery system to the citizens. This will also aim at creating transparent government so as to fulfil the citizens charter.

IT developments in State Government would be through the following stages:

(a) For each department, identification of key area on priority basis needs to be computerised first. The criterion would be computerising those systems first which improve the delivery systems for the citizens. This includes ration card, driving licence NA permission, Sales-tax Return etc. This is only an indicative list.

(b) By completing these data base in a time-bound fashion and making them operational, delivery time for the citizens will have to be cut down demonstrably in a time-bound fashion.

(c) To create greater convenience for the citizens, it would be imperative to create efficient/intelligent interface, which can take form of computer-supported counters, Kiosks, etc. The government would strive to ensure that all the forms required to be filled in by citizens for interface with the government would be available for filling in electronically by the year 2005. Prior to this, citizens will have access to forms through Kiosks/other vendors by way of electronic devices. This would be achieved by the year 2002 AD. Choices for the citizens to obtain and complete forms by means other than electronic would also be kept open.

The system of information Kiosks would be the major integrators of various databases existing with various Government departments. Government will bring suitable legislation to guarantee protection of citizens related information which would be existing on various databases.

In order to ensure that there is no duplication of data entry and thereby to avoid confusion, the State government would issue multi-purpose cards to all citizens of the State. These would be in the form of suitable smart cards. This will ensure security to individual information and would also provide one point coding system.

Enabling Mechanism

1. All departments will prepare there IT Action Plan, which would have a one-year focus and a five-year perspective.
2. One per cent of the State Government budget would be committed to IT related activities which is expected to rise to 3 per cent in the year 2005 AD.
3. To ensure quicker availability of funds, a separate IT sub-head would be created within each major head. IT related funds will not be subject to any economy measures and they would be made available as far as practicable in lump sum to the departmental heads rather than in the form of quarterly/ monthly releases.
4. To oversee implementation of IT strategies in the departments, each department will have Chief Information Officer (CIO) who would report directly to Secretary of the department. Considering the nature of mobility of IT professionals, such CIO would be recruited on contractual basis and recruitment would be freed from encumbrances of Gujarat Public Service Commission (GPSC).
5. All departments would create shareable databases of rules and other related information. This would include information such as budget, recruitment/service rules, plan achievements for various schemes etc.

6. Creation of E-mail system.
7. Creation of document imaging system to reduce paper work.
8. Each department will create web page within the State Government web-site to display grievance-handling procedure. By the year 2001 AD, facility would be provided to citizens for their grievances to be handled electronically as well.
9. Certain inter-departmental projects which have considerable significance as being underlying feature for all other IT related activities as well as of considerable importance for the well being of the citizens of the State would be given a special status of State IT Projects. This would include projects such as disaster management system, citizens database, budget etc. Inter-departmental committee to be appointed hereafter would monitor them.

Amendment in the Policy guidelines for imparting Computer Training to government personnel through empanelled training institutions

Government of Gujarat General Administration Department
G.R. No. ITP-1099-434-ITD-(Part-I),
Dated: 15-2-2001

Preamble

The government had empanelled Computer Training Institutions *vide* GR referred to in above at Sr. No. (1) dated 9-9-99 and laid down the guidelines for imparting computer training to the government employees.

After reviewing the performance it was felt that additional training institutes be empanelled for giving training to employees in all government offices. Accordingly, a committee was framed *vide* G.R. dated 31-5-2000 (read (3) above) for empanelling additional training institutes. The committee submitted its report to the State Government on 22-8-2000. The Committee recommended that training targets be fixed for each institute and their performance be reviewed regularly by all departments. Based on these recommendations government is pleased to amend the G.R. of 9-9-99.

Amendment

(1) G.R. dated 9-9-99 read in (1) above is amended as below. In Para (1) B following Institutes are added with a minimum total targetted personnel to be trained within six month as below:

*****

(4) In addition to this, the institutes having DOEACC (Department of Electronics Accreditation of Computer Courses) or IETE (Institute of Electronics and Telecommunication Engineers) accreditations will be considered for imparting training to government employees with prior permission of Information Technology Division, General Administration Department.

Madhya Pradesh

VISION—Seamless Society with Global Opportunities

The vision statement for the State's IT Policy is the creation of a "Seamless Society with Global Opportunities". The Statement implies that there should be no islands of elitism or conclaves of wisdom in the information society of the future-where access to information and knowledge would be symmetric among all seekers and users. Every citizen must feel comfortable in accessing information through the facility of technology—whether directly or where essential through public or private intermediaries. It is to create such a confident society of the future that human resources should be developed in the State.

The State has set a target of providing information access to all citizens at an affordable cost and for achieving IT literacy in all the high schools and colleges by the year 2003 and aims to do so in all the schools by the year 2008. IT penetration would be achieved through aiming for an optimistic average of one internet connection per 100 population and coverage of every habitat by 2003.

Computerisation in government departments and agencies must be the engine of growth of IT in Madhya Pradesh, in the initial period. An optimistic goal for computer penetration in the government, its organisations including the Panchayat Raj Institutions and other local self-government institutions has been kept at one per ten employees by the year 2003, raised to one per five employees by the year 2005 and finally to one per two employees by the year 2008.

The objectives of Madhya Pradesh Agency for Promotion of Information Technology (MAP-IT) would be the following:

- To propel the growth of Information Technology (IT) in Madhya Pradesh and implementation of the State IT Action Plan for socio-economic development of the state.
- To coordinate with all the government departments and agencies for sectoral and cross-sectoral promotion and use of IT in Government and prescribe guidelines to enable smooth and widespread induction of IT.
- Coordinate and Network with investors and Industry, Trade organisations and financial institutions in public and private sector to promote growth in IT sector.
- To generate awareness amongst citizens and demystification of IT so as to promote its use as a comprehensive and cost effective means of disseminating information.
- Coordinate manpower needs and human resource development efforts for the above objectives.
- Coordinate and pursue development of all support infrastructure including telecom infrastructure in the State with the State Government and the Government of India and their agencies.
- Marketing the State as an attractive IT destination for investment.
- Identifying and developing opportunities for furthering

innovative research of world standard on its own or in collaboration with one or more institutions and/or industry.

Hindi is the medium of communication among governments and the population over the largest landmass of India. All the web pages of government departments would also be in Hindi to increase their reach. The use of Hindi would also be promoted in all IT based databases and applications. Further, necessary action would be taken towards the following:

- To make Hindi e-mail as an important medium of communication between departments and field level offices.
- To ensure that in all public purchases of hardware/software, the systems being procured would have bilingual capabilities, e.g. all keyboards would be bilingual facilitating.
- Partnering the Hindi language news papers and other media organisations based in the State for popularisation, dissemination as well as access to Hindi formats.
- Collaboration with the other Hindi speaking States such as U.P., Bihar, Rajasthan, Delhi and H.P. for a joint programme of promoting Hindi's presence on the internet by uploading and enhancing Hindi resources. Easy availability of standardised fonts would be part of this exercise.
- Collaboration with C-DAC for the setting up of an institute and research centre of world standing for addressing problems relating to use of IT in Hindi computing in these languages, promotion of software applications in the vernacular, etc.

IT cannot grow in isolation to the general pace and status of economic development of the State and so the IT policy will be dovetailed, giving it the pride of place in the Industrial Policy of the State. Commercial tax administration would provide opportunities for such incentives by accepting computerised tax returns, encouragement to computerised billing, bar coding of inventory etc.

Promotion of IT in Government

IT Sub-plans: The annual plan of each department/sector in Government would have a detailed sub-plan for IT. Every department would be required to establish IT working group consisting of senior officers and representative of employees, a representative from MAP-IT, and also co-opting IT professionals on voluntary or contractual basis from other departments or agencies. There would be a nodal officer or executive for IT related matters in every department.

Budgetary outlay: A distinct budgetary head of account for IT related activities would be introduced in the annual budget from this fiscal year.

The State Government would impress upon the XI Central Finance Commission the need to modernise administration at the level of State Government as well as at the level of the PRIs. Additionally, modernisation and computerisation of systems in the Panchayats, would be included in the list of priorities for grants given as per the recommendations of the State Finance Commission.

The financial resources for computer penetration for Gram Panchayats presently numbering 31,126 would be met out of the grants-in-aid for basic services, and/or by financing one educated unemployed Youth/Panchayat Karmi at each Gram Panchayat HQ to own/operate a computer unit for various value added services including information retailing through kiosks.

An action plan would be prepared to ensure that all offices of the district government including those at the sub-district levels are computerised and networked by the year 2003. In particular, the tehsil offices dealing with land records, revenue legislation, land acquisition information, collection and allocation of land revenue and cess to Panchayats, payments of compensation, planning an execution and expenditure on relief operations, information on listing of revenue court cases, monitoring of progress in disposal of revenue case work etc. would be taken up for computerisation by year 2003. Offices such as those of the district governments and the PRIs should be in a position to enable single window facilitation after computerisation.

E-mail facility would be extended to all employees to encourage greater use of email facility for communication.

The *mantra* for introduction of IT in Government departments would be Zero additional personnel costs, except costs on training and re-tooling of the serving employees. The present pace of training would be stepped up to match computer penetration goals.

A special scheme of incentives would be introduced to motivate all Government employees to become computer literate. To do so in the shortest possible timeframe, there would be a strategy of contracting with public and private sector training institutes for specially designed short-term courses for different groups of users.

All hardware supplies would be contracted with a compulsory clause on familiarisation of employees in the operations. All bulk procurement of generic software as well as contracts on specialised application software development would be out-sourced on similar conditionalities for training.

Proposal to tie up with banks for hire purchase schemes for the employees and provide interest-subsidy for purchase of computers for personal use by employees would be worked out.

All departments will move towards electronic communication within the department. Necessary changes in the office manuals would be worked out for this purpose.

Networks: Every department would establish a LAN by the year 2003. The district government offices, the Collectorate and the Zila Panchayats as well as all other large offices would also establish respective intra-office networks.

The State unit of NIC provides a wide range of IT services in Madhya Pradesh. The NICNET facility has enabled networking with the districts and creation of many information systems and databases in various departments/sectors. These systems/databases would be upscaled and/or augmented and made on-line seamlessly. Detailed plans would be prepared especially in respect of the following:

(i) The Agriculture Market Information System on commodity arrivals and price movements in the major mandies.

(ii) The Treasury Accounting Information System.
(iii) The Commercial Taxes Information System.
(iv) The databases under the DISNIC-PLAN. Village Information System and Gram Sampark Abhiyan.
(v) The Transport Management System.

The schedule for implementation of IT based systems in Government departments would be in phases.

Creation of a Citizen Database: A unique social security ID number would be introduced for those availing various benefits such as social assistance, social security pension etc. The BPL household survey, survey conducted for electoral photo identity cards, etc. would form the database for such an exercise to improve delivery of services and eliminate leakage.

Manpower Development for IT

Training for Government Employees: Training efforts, which are at present confined to largely the NIC initiative, would be multiplied. The existing Training institutions for the training of employees of the various departments as well as the State Academy of Administration would be upgraded to meet the requirements. Training tie up with private institutes using a common modular training package would also be used for re-tooling of employees.

Employees engaged in course studies in IT through distance education or other certification programmes would be allowed to use office computers after work hours. Recognition of computer time thus spent would be given due credit by the institutions awarding certificates.

To meet the manpower needs of the State in IT, private sector training institutions, and distance education format would also be encouraged along with other Government supported institutions.

For demystification of IT and computers, the State Council of Education Research and Training would develop and include course material of an elementary nature to arouse curiosity and satisfy young minds at the primary school level.

Madhya Pradesh would aim at creating computer awareness among its masses of a magnitude far higher and not yet achieved or aimed by any other State. It would be universal in character. Only then can people benefit from the IT policy and drive up demand for IT in the State as also throw up the trained manpower. In the ultimate analysis people must feel comfortable in using technology.

References

Abramson, J. B., Christopher A. F. & Orren, G. R. (1988). *The electronic commonwealth: The impact of new media technologies on democratic politics.* New York: Basic Books.

Abramson, M. A. & Means, G. E. (Eds.). (2001). *E-Government 2001*. Oxford: Rowman and Littlefield Publishers, Inc.

Alexander, C. J. & Pal, L. A. (1998). *Digital Democracy: Policy and Politics in the Wired World.* Oxford: Oxford University Press.

Barber, B. (1998). Three scenarios for the future of technology and strong democracy. *Political Science Quarterly, 113*(4), 573-589.

Beierle, T. C. (2002). "Engaging the public through online policy dialogues". Paper Presented at the Prospects for Electronic Democracy Conference, Carnegie Mellon University, Pittsburgh, Pennsylvania.

Bovens, M. & Zouridis, S. (2002). From street-level to system-level bureaucracies: How information and communication technology is transforming administrative discretion and constitution control. *Public Administration Review, 62*(2), 174-184.

Coe, A., Paquet, G. and Roy, J. (2001). E-governance and smart communities: A social learning challenge. *Social Science Computer Review, 19*(1), 80-93.

Compaine, B. M., (Ed.). (2001). *The digital divide: Facing a crisis or creating a myth?* Cambridge, MA: MIT Press.

Danziger, J. N. & Andersen, K. (2002). Impacts of information technology on public administration: An analysis of empirical research from the 'golden age' of transformation. *International Journal of Public Administration, 25*(5), 591-627.

Editorial, Information Technology in Developing Countries—Volume 11, No. 3, December 2001 Newsletter of IFIP Working Group 9.4 and Commonwealth Network for Information Technology.

Etzioni, A. & Etzioni, O. (1999). Face-to-face and computer-mediated communities, a comparative analysis. *Information Society, 15*(4), 241-248.

Heeks, Richard—Understanding e-Governance for Development—Working Paper No. 11/2001 of Institute for Development Policy and Management, University of Manchester.

Kamarck, Elaine Ciulla & Joseph S. Nye, Jr., (Eds.). 1999. *Democracy.com? Governance in a Networked World.* Hollis: Hollis Publishing.

Kate Oakley—What is e-Governance? (2002) Paper presented in E-Governance Workshop at Strasbourg on 10-11 June, 2002.

Kulchitsky, D. Roman—Cargo Cults, Knowledge, and IT-for-Decision-Making Strategies in Developing Countries.

Norris, P. (Ed.). (1999). *Critical citizens: Global support for democratic government.* Cambridge: Oxford University Press.

O'Looney, J. A. (2002). *Wiring governments: Challenges and possibilities for public managers.* Westport: Quorum Books.

Peters, B. G. (1996). *The future of governing: Four emerging models.* Lawrence, Kansas: University Press of Kansas.

Scavo, C. and Shi, Y. (2000). The role of information technology in the reinventing government paradigm: Normative predicates and practical challenges. *Social Science Computer Review, 18*(2), 166-178.

Thaha, A. and Vijayadharan, D. (2001) I T Landscape in India: Focus: Agriculture and Rural Development: Centre for Rural and Urban Studies and Training (CRUST), Hyderabad.

Web References

http://egov.mit.gov.in/

http://planningcommission.nic.in/

http://www.upgov.nic.in/

http://www.upportal.com/

http://www.allahabadhighcourt.nic.in/

http://bihar.nic.in/

http://www.wbgov.com/e-gov/English/EnglishHomePage.asp

http://www.aponline.gov.in/apportal/userinterface/information/SDPLocationWiseList.aspx

http://www.aponline.gov.in/apportal/departments/listofOrgsbyDepts.asp

http://www.aponline.gov.in/Quick%20Links/events/Services%20Launch/eSavaAponline.html

http://www.aponline.gov.in/apportal/lifecycle/lifecycle_ie.html

http://www.aponline.gov.in/apportal/webdirectory/webdirectory.aspx

http://www.ap.gov.in/card/

http://arunachalpradesh.nic.in/

http://assamgovt.nic.in/
http://assamgovt.nic.in/itpolassam.htm
http://assamgovt.nic.in/itassam.htm
http://mizoram.nic.in/
http://www.tn.gov.in/
http://www.ap.gov.in/AP-Sites/twins/twin.htm
http://kar.nic.in/
http://www.kar.nic.in/nitpu/
http://www.maharashtra.gov.in/
http://www.mp.nic.in/dit/itinit.htm
http://www.mp.nic.in/dit/policy.htm
http://www.mpgovt.nic.in/index/cindex.htm#it
http://www.gujaratindia.com/
http://www.gujaratindia.com/Initiative/Initiative2.htm
http://haryana.nic.in/
http://punjabgovt.nic.in/government/government.htm
http://www1.worldbank.org/publicsector/egov/
http://www1.worldbank.org/publicsector/egov/egovstudies.htm
http://www.unpan.org/dpepa-kmb-eg-egovranda-ready.asp
http://www1.worldbank.org/publicsector/egov/bhoomi_cs.htm

Index